International VAT/GST Guidelines

This work is published under the responsibility of the Secretary-General of the OECD. The opinions expressed and arguments employed herein do not necessarily reflect the official views of OECD member countries.

This document and any map included herein are without prejudice to the status of or sovereignty over any territory, to the delimitation of international frontiers and boundaries and to the name of any territory, city or area.

Please cite this publication as:
OECD (2017), *International VAT/GST Guidelines*, OECD Publishing, Paris.
http://dx.doi.org/10.1787/9789264271401-en

ISBN 978-92-64-27204-0 (print)
ISBN 978-92-64-27140-1 (PDF)
ISBN 978-92-64-27146-3 (ePub)

The statistical data for Israel are supplied by and under the responsibility of the relevant Israeli authorities. The use of such data by the OECD is without prejudice to the status of the Golan Heights, East Jerusalem and Israeli settlements in the West Bank under the terms of international law.

Photo credits: © iStockphoto.com/Maxiphoto.

Corrigenda to OECD publications may be found on line at: *www.oecd.org/about/publishing/corrigenda.htm*.

© OECD 2017

Foreword

T he International VAT/GST Guidelines[1] ("the Guidelines") set forth internationally agreed principles and standards for the value added tax (VAT) treatment of the most common types of international transactions, with a particular focus on trade in services and intangibles. Their aim is to minimise inconsistencies in the application of VAT in a cross-border context with a view to reducing uncertainty and risks of double taxation and unintended non-taxation in international trade. They also include the recommended principles and mechanisms to address the challenges for the collection of VAT on cross-border sales of digital products that had been identified in the context of the OECD/G20 Project on Base and Erosion and Profit Shifting (the BEPS Project).[2] VAT is a major source of revenue for governments around the world. Some 165 countries operated a VAT at the time of completion of these Guidelines, more than twice as many as 25 years before. This global spread of the VAT coincided with the rapid expansion of the international trade in goods and services in an increasingly globalised economy. Most international trade is now subject to VAT and the interaction of national VAT regimes can potentially have a major impact in either facilitating or distorting trade. The absence of an internationally agreed framework for the application of VAT to cross-border trade created growing risks of under-taxation and loss of revenue for governments, and of trade distortion due to double taxation. This had become especially problematic with respect to international trade in services and intangibles, which has shown a particularly strong growth notably as a consequence of the expansion of the digital economy.

Against this background, the OECD Committee on Fiscal Affairs (CFA) launched the project to develop the International VAT/GST Guidelines in 2006, recognising that jurisdictions would benefit from an internationally agreed standard that contributes towards ensuring that VAT systems interact consistently so that they facilitate rather than distort international trade. These Guidelines were intended to set the standard for countries when designing and administering their domestic rules.

The International VAT/GST Guidelines build on international dialogue among OECD Members and partner countries and other relevant stakeholders, including academia and private institutions. Recognising the growing need to further strengthen the involvement of partner economies in the development of the Guidelines, the CFA created the Global Forum on VAT in 2012 as a platform for a structured VAT policy dialogue with partner countries and other relevant stakeholders. The meetings of this Global Forum provided the opportunity for countries worldwide, particularly developing economies, to contribute actively to the development of the Guidelines. At its first *meeting on 7-8 November 2012, this Global Forum agreed that the Guidelines should be the basis for the much needed global standard on the application of VAT to the international trade in services and intangibles and that the Global Forum's key objective would be to build the widest possible international consensus on these Guidelines with a view to achieving their endorsement as the international standard*

The Guidelines were completed in 2015. In November 2015, at the third meeting of the Global Forum on VAT, the high-level officials of the participating 104 jurisdictions and international organisations endorsed the Guidelines as a global standard for the VAT treatment of international trade in services and intangibles to serve as a reference point for designing and implementing legislation. All Global Forum participants welcomed the active involvement of an increasing number of countries worldwide and of the global business community in shaping the outcomes of this work. They also welcomed the prospect of the incorporation of these Guidelines into an OECD Council Recommendation that would be open to adherence by all interested partner economies.

The Guidelines were incorporated in the Recommendation on the Application of Value Added Tax/Goods and Services Tax to the International Trade in Services and Intangibles, which was adopted by the Council of the OECD on 27 September 2016 (included in the Appendix of this publication). This Recommendation is the first OECD legal instrument in the area of VAT and the first internationally agreed framework for the application of VAT to cross-border trade which aspires to a global coverage.

This Recommendation is addressed to Members and to non-Members having adhered to it ("Adherents"). It represents these jurisdictions' political will on the application of VAT to the international trade in services and intangibles with a view to addressing the risks of double taxation and unintended non-taxation that result from the uncoordinated application of VAT in a cross-border context. They are encouraged to take due account of the Guidelines when designing and implementing VAT legislation. They are in particular encouraged to pursue efforts to implement the principles of VAT neutrality and the principles of destination for determining the place of taxation of cross-border supplies with a view to facilitating a coherent application of national VAT legislation to international trade.

Notes

1. *The terms "value added tax" and "VAT" are used to refer to any national tax by whatever name or acronym it is known such as Goods and Services Tax (GST) that embodies the basic features of a value added tax, i.e. a broad-based tax on final consumption collected from, but in principle not borne by, businesses through a staged collection process, whatever method is used for determining the tax liability (e.g. invoice-credit method or subtraction method).*

2. *These recommended principles and mechanisms were also included in the Final Report on OECD/G20 BEPS Action 1 "Addressing the Tax Challenges of the Digital Economy". This Report was endorsed by the OECD Council on 1 October and was endorsed by G20 Leaders during their Summit in Antalya on 15-16 November 2015.*

Table of contents

Follow OECD Publications on:

 http://twitter.com/OECD_Pubs

 http://www.facebook.com/OECDPublications

 http://www.linkedin.com/groups/OECD-Publications-4645871

 http://www.youtube.com/oecdilibrary

 http://www.oecd.org/oecddirect/

Preface

1.   As Value Added Tax ("VAT")[1] has continued to spread across the world, international trade in goods and services has likewise expanded rapidly in an increasingly globalised economy. One consequence of these developments has been the greater interaction between VAT systems, along with growing risks of double taxation and unintended non-taxation in the absence of international VAT coordination.

2.   Basic VAT principles are generally the same across jurisdictions insofar as they are designed to tax final consumption in the jurisdiction where it occurs according to the destination principle. Nevertheless, since the late 1990s tax authorities and the business community have recognised that VAT rules require greater coherence to avoid burdens on global trade. They have also recognised that a co-operative approach is required to solve common problems.

3.   The first tangible output of the OECD's work in this area came with the 1998 Ottawa Conference on electronic commerce which endorsed the *Ottawa Taxation Framework Conditions*. Building on this work, the OECD's Committee on Fiscal Affairs ("CFA") adopted the *Guidelines on Consumption Taxation of Cross-Border Services and Intangible Property in the Context of E-commerce* (2003), which were complemented by the *Consumption Tax Guidance Series* (2003).

4.   Against the background of the strong growth of international trade in services, evidence grew that tax issues needing attention were not confined to electronic commerce but that VAT could distort cross-border trade in services and intangibles more generally and that this situation was creating obstacles to business activity, hindering economic growth and distorting competition. Recognising that jurisdictions would benefit from principles that contribute toward ensuring that VAT systems interact consistently so that they facilitate rather than distort international trade, the OECD launched a project to develop *International VAT/GST Guidelines* ("the Guidelines").

---

1. For ease of reading, the terms "value added tax" and "VAT" are used to refer to any national tax that embodies the basic features of a value added tax as described in Chapter 1, by whatever name or acronym it is known [e.g. "Goods and Services Tax" ("GST")].

The International VAT/GST Guidelines: Aim and status

5.   The Guidelines set forth a number of principles for the VAT treatment of the most common types of international transactions, focusing on trade in services and intangibles, with the aim of reducing the uncertainty and risks of double taxation and unintended non-taxation that result from inconsistencies in the application of VAT in a cross-border context. The Guidelines build on international dialogue among OECD Members and Partners and other relevant stakeholders, including academia and private institutions.

6.   The Guidelines do not aim at detailed prescriptions for national legislation. Jurisdictions are sovereign with respect to the design and application of their laws. Rather, the Guidelines seek to identify objectives and suggest means for achieving them. Their purpose is to serve as a reference point. They are intended to assist policy makers in their efforts to evaluate and develop the legal and administrative framework in their jurisdictions, taking into account their specific economic, legal, institutional, cultural and social circumstances and practices.

7.   The Guidelines are evolutionary in nature and should be reviewed in light of relevant developments. Governments have an important responsibility for shaping effective tax frameworks, thereby assessing the likely effects, costs and benefits of policy options and ensuring sufficient flexibility to respond to evolving circumstances and demands. Such developments may call for further updating and revision of the Guidelines.

8.   The Guidelines apply only to VAT systems, by whatever name or acronym they are known, that embody the basic features described in Chapter 1: broad-based taxes on final consumption collected from, but in principle not borne by, businesses through a staged collection process (by whatever approach, e.g. invoice-credit method or subtraction method). In principle, taxes that lack these characteristics fall outside the scope of the Guidelines, even if they are denominated as a type of VAT. For example a production-type VAT would not be covered because such a tax is not designed to tax final consumption. The Guidelines also do not apply to single-stage consumption taxes charged only once to the end user at the final point of sale, such as retail sales taxes.

Development process of the International VAT/GST Guidelines

9.   The Guidelines have been developed by the CFA, through its Working Party No. 9 on Consumption Taxes, in co-operation with a number of Partner countries and the Working Party's Technical Advisory Group ("TAG"), consisting of representatives from tax authorities, international organisations and business, and further supported by academics. The core features of the VAT, as described in Chapter 1, imply that businesses play an important role in the collection of the tax. Although they should not, in principle, bear the

burden of the tax, businesses inevitably bear compliance costs associated with the collection of the tax at all intermediary stages of the supply chain up to the final consumer and with the remittance to the tax authorities. Businesses are therefore considered key partners for jurisdictions in designing and operating VAT systems and the business community is actively involved in the development of the Guidelines.

10.   The Guidelines have been developed in a staged process and the CFA regularly published interim drafts for public consultation. When the process of consultation was completed, all comments were carefully considered and the drafts were modified when appropriate. Work then continued on the basis of the progress achieved. Each element of the Guidelines was regarded as a building block and was reviewed in the light of the subsequent contributions to the Guidelines in order to form a coherent whole.

11.   In addition to the core features of the VAT described in Chapter 1, the Guidelines as currently constituted address the fundamental principles of VAT that apply to cross-border trade, i.e. the neutrality of the tax (see Chapter 2); the definition of the place of taxation for cross-border trade in services and intangibles[2] between businesses ("business-to-business supplies") and between businesses and final consumers ("business-to-consumer supplies") (see Chapter 3); and mechanisms for supporting the Guidelines in practice, including mutual co-operation, dispute minimisation, and application in cases of evasion and avoidance (see Chapter 4).

12.   Underpinning these Guidelines is the assumption that parties involved act in good faith and that all supplies are legitimate and with economic substance. Chapter 4 provides guidance on the application of the Guidelines in cases of evasion and avoidance.

---

2. Some jurisdictions have categories of supplies other than goods and services. For ease of reference, in these Guidelines items such as intellectual property rights and other intangibles are referred to as "intangibles".

Chapter 1

Core features of value added taxes

1.1   This Chapter describes the core features of VAT, with a particular focus on their application to international trade. The description is based on widely shared understandings among tax administrations, businesses, academics, and other tax experts regarding the VAT's overall purpose, design, and implementation.

A. Overarching purpose of a VAT: A broad-based tax on final consumption

1.2   The overarching purpose of a VAT is to impose a broad-based tax on consumption, which is understood to mean final consumption by households. In principle only private individuals, as distinguished from businesses, engage in the consumption at which a VAT is targeted. In practice, however, many VAT systems impose VAT burden not only on consumption by private individuals, but also on various entities that are involved in non-business activities.

1.3   As a broad-based tax, the VAT is distinguishable from excises targeted at specific forms of consumption such as the purchase of gasoline or alcohol.

1.4   A necessary consequence of the fundamental proposition that a VAT is a tax on final consumption by households is that the burden of the VAT should not rest on businesses. This follows as a matter of elementary logic from the proposition that the VAT is a tax on household consumption, because businesses are not households and, at least as a matter of principle, are incapable of final or household consumption. In practice, if a business acquires goods, services or intangibles that are used in whole or in part for the private consumption of the business owners, VAT regimes must determine whether, or the extent to which, the purchase should be treated as acquired for business purposes or for private consumption.

B. The central design feature of a VAT: Staged collection process

1.5   The central design feature of a VAT, and the feature from which it derives its name, is that the tax is collected through a staged process. Each business in the supply chain takes part in the process of controlling and collecting the tax, remitting the proportion of tax corresponding to its margin, i.e. on the difference between the VAT imposed on its taxed inputs and the VAT imposed on its taxed outputs. Thus, the tax is in principle collected on the "value added" at each stage of production and distribution. In this respect, the VAT differs from a retail sales tax ("RST"), which taxes consumption through a single-stage levy imposed in theory only at the point of final sale.

1.6   This central design feature of the VAT, coupled with the fundamental principle that the burden of the tax should not rest on businesses, requires a mechanism for relieving businesses of the burden of the VAT they pay when they acquire goods, services, or intangibles. There are two principal approaches to implementing the staged collection process while relieving businesses of the VAT burden, thus permitting successive taxpayers to deduct the VAT they pay on their purchases while accounting for the VAT they collect on their sales. Under the invoice-credit method (which is a "transaction based method"), each trader charges VAT at the rate specified for each supply and passes to the purchaser an invoice showing the amount of tax charged. The purchaser is in turn able to credit that input tax against the output tax charged on its sales, remitting the balance to the tax authorities and receiving refunds when there are excess credits. Under the subtraction method (which is an "entity based method"), the tax is levied directly on an accounts-based measure of value added, which is determined for each business by subtracting the VAT calculated on allowable purchases from the VAT calculated on taxable supplies. Almost all jurisdictions that operate a VAT use the invoice-credit method.

1.7   In general, OECD jurisdictions with a VAT impose the tax at every stage of the economic process and allow deduction of taxes on purchases by all but the final consumer. This design feature gives to the VAT its essential character in domestic trade as an economically neutral tax. The full right to deduct input tax through the supply chain, except by the final consumer, ensures the neutrality of the tax, whatever the nature of the product, the structure of the distribution chain, and the means used for its delivery (e.g. retail stores, physical delivery, Internet downloads). As a result of the staged payment system, VAT thereby "flows through the businesses" to tax supplies made to final consumers.

C. VAT and international trade: The destination principle

1.8   The overarching purpose of VAT as a levy on final consumption, coupled with its central design feature of a staged collection process, lays the foundation for the core VAT principles bearing on international trade. The fundamental issue of economic policy in relation to the international application of the VAT is whether the levy should be imposed by the jurisdiction of origin or destination. Under the destination principle, tax is ultimately levied only on the final consumption that occurs within the taxing jurisdiction. Under the origin principle, the tax is levied in the various jurisdictions where the value was added. The key economic difference between the two principles is that the destination principle places all firms competing in a given jurisdiction on an even footing whereas the origin principle places consumers in different jurisdictions on an even footing.

1.9   The application of the destination principle in VAT achieves neutrality in international trade. Under the destination principle, exports are not subject to tax with refund of input taxes (that is, "free of VAT" or "zero-rated") and imports are taxed on the same basis and at the same rates as domestic supplies. Accordingly, the total tax paid in relation to a supply is determined by the rules applicable in the jurisdiction of its consumption and all revenue accrues to the jurisdiction where the supply to the final consumer occurs.

1.10   By contrast, under the origin principle each jurisdiction would levy VAT on the value created within its own borders.[3] Under an origin-based regime, exporting jurisdictions would tax exports on the same basis and at the same rate as domestic supplies, while importing jurisdictions would give a credit against their own VAT for the hypothetical tax that would have been paid at the importing jurisdiction's own rate. Tax paid on a supply would then reflect the pattern of its origins and the aggregate revenue would be distributed in that pattern. This would run counter to the core features of a VAT: as a tax on consumption, the revenue should accrue to the jurisdiction where the final consumption takes place. Under the origin principle, these revenues are shared amongst jurisdictions where value is added. By imposing tax at the various rates applicable in the jurisdictions where value is added, the origin principle could influence the economic or geographical structure of the value chain and undermine neutrality in international trade.

1.11   For these reasons, there is widespread consensus that the destination principle, with revenue accruing to the country of import where final consumption occurs, is preferable to the origin principle from both a theoretical and practical standpoint. In fact, the destination principle is the international norm and is sanctioned by World Trade Organization ("WTO") rules.[4]

1.12   Because of the widespread acceptance of the destination principle for applying VAT to international trade, most of the rules currently in force are generally intended to tax supplies of goods, services and intangibles within the jurisdiction where consumption takes place. Practical means of implementing this intention are, nevertheless, diverse across jurisdictions, which can in some instances lead to double taxation or unintended non-taxation, and to uncertainties for both businesses and tax administrations.

---

3. This should be distinguished from the term used in the European Union for a proposed system (which was not implemented) in which the VAT would have been collected by the Member State of origin and the revenue later channelled to the Member State of destination for transactions within the European Union.
4. Footnote 1 of the WTO's Agreement on Subsidies and Countervailing Measures provides that "… the exemption of an exported product from duties or taxes borne by the like product when destined for domestic consumption, or the remission of such duties or taxes in amounts not in excess of those which have accrued, shall not be deemed to be a subsidy."

1.13   Implementation of the destination principle with respect to international trade in goods is relatively straightforward in theory and generally effective in practice, due in large part to the existence of border controls or fiscal frontiers. When a transaction involves goods being moved from one jurisdiction to another, the goods are generally taxed where they are delivered. The exported goods are free of VAT in the seller's jurisdiction (and are freed of any residual VAT via successive businesses' deductions of input tax), whilst imports are subject to the same VAT as equivalent domestic goods in the purchaser's jurisdiction. The VAT on imports is generally collected at the same time as customs duties, although in some jurisdictions collection is postponed until declared on the importer's next VAT return. Allowing deduction of the VAT incurred at importation in the same way as input tax deduction on a domestic supply ensures neutrality and limits distortions in relation to international trade.

1.14   Implementing the destination principle for international trade in services and intangibles is more difficult than for international trade in goods. The nature of services and intangibles is such that they cannot be subject to border controls in the same way as goods. For these reasons, Guidelines have been developed for determining the jurisdiction of taxation for international supplies of services and intangibles that reflect the destination principle (see Chapter 3).

1.15   Making exports free of VAT and taxing imports introduce a breach in the staged collection process. In many VAT systems that operate an invoice-credit method, the VAT on cross-border business-to-business supplies of services and intangibles is collected by the reverse charge mechanism. This is a tax mechanism that switches the liability to pay the tax from the supplier to the customer. In the absence of such a mechanism, foreign suppliers that deliver services in jurisdictions where they are not established would in principle have to register for VAT purposes and fulfil all VAT obligations in these jurisdictions. To avoid such administrative burdens on foreign suppliers, and to assure that VAT is accounted for, the reverse charge mechanism allows (or sometimes requires) the VAT registered customer to account for the tax on supplies received from foreign suppliers. If the customer is entitled to a full input tax credit in respect of the supply, it may be that local VAT legislation does not require the reverse charge to be made. However, the reverse charge mechanism is not applied in all jurisdictions and, where it is implemented, the rules may differ from country to country.

D. Application of generally accepted principles of tax policy to VAT: The Ottawa Taxation Framework Conditions

1.16   Although they were articulated in the context of taxation of electronic commerce, the generally accepted principles of tax policy applicable to consumption taxes that were welcomed by Ministers from across the globe in

1998[5] are broadly applicable to VATs in both domestic and international trade. Indeed, the *Ottawa Taxation Framework Conditions* themselves derived from the "same principles that governments apply to taxation of conventional commerce."[6] These generally accepted principles of tax policy, some of which have already been noted above, are as follows:

- **Neutrality:** Taxation should seek to be neutral and equitable between forms of electronic commerce and between conventional and electronic forms of commerce. Business decisions should be motivated by economic rather than tax considerations. Taxpayers in similar situations carrying out similar transactions should be subject to similar levels of taxation.

- **Efficiency:** Compliance costs for businesses and administrative costs for the tax authorities should be minimised as far as possible.

- **Certainty and simplicity:** The tax rules should be clear and simple to understand so that taxpayers can anticipate the tax consequences in advance of a transaction, including knowing when, where, and how the tax is to be accounted.

- **Effectiveness and fairness:** Taxation should produce the right amount of tax at the right time. The potential for tax evasion and avoidance should be minimised while keeping counteracting measures proportionate to risks involved.

- **Flexibility:** The systems for taxation should be flexible and dynamic to ensure that they keep pace with technological and commercial developments.

1.17   While these tax policy principles guide the development of the *International VAT/GST Guidelines* in general, Chapter 2 of these Guidelines is specifically dedicated to neutrality given its importance as a core principle of VAT design.

---

5. The Ottawa Taxation Framework Conditions were welcomed by Ministers at the Ministerial Conference on Electronic Commerce held in Ottawa on 7-9 October 1998.
6. OECD (2001), Taxation and Electronic Commerce – Implementing the Ottawa Taxation Framework Conditions, OECD, Paris.

Chapter 2

Neutrality of value added taxes in the context of cross-border trade

A. Introduction

2.1   The concept of tax neutrality in VAT has a number of dimensions, including the absence of discrimination in a tax environment that is unbiased and impartial and the elimination of undue tax burdens and disproportionate or inappropriate compliance costs for businesses. Neutrality is one of the principles that help to ensure the collection of the right amount of revenue by governments.

2.2   These Guidelines are concerned with all aspects of neutrality in the international context. Although they draw from the basic principles that apply to domestic transactions, they do not cover domestic aspects of neutrality, such as the influence of the tax structure (e.g. different rates and exemptions) on decisions by consumers.

B. Basic neutrality principles

2.3   The basic principles underpinning neutrality are set out in Chapter 1. In domestic trade, tax neutrality is achieved in principle by the multi-stage payment system: each business pays VAT to its providers on its inputs and receives VAT from its customers on its outputs. To ensure that the "right" amount of tax is remitted to tax authorities, input VAT incurred by each business is offset against its output VAT, resulting in a liability to pay the net amount or balance of those two.[7] This means that VAT normally "flows through the business" to tax the final consumers. It is therefore important that at each stage, the supplier be entitled to a full right of deduction of input tax, so that the tax burden eventually rests on the final consumer rather than on the intermediaries in the supply chain. This principle is laid down in Guideline 2.1.

Guideline 2.1

The burden of value added taxes themselves should not lie on taxable businesses except where explicitly provided for in legislation.

---

7. In some cases, the result of the offset gives rise to a refund due by the tax authorities to the business. Examples include businesses that incur more tax on their inputs than is due on their outputs (such as exporters, whose output is free of VAT in their jurisdiction under the destination principle) and businesses whose purchases are larger than their sales in the same period (such as new or developing businesses and seasonal businesses).

2.4   In this context, the words "except where explicitly provided" mean that jurisdictions may legitimately place a value added tax burden on business. The following examples illustrate a number of situations where this is the case:

- Where transactions made by businesses are exempt because the tax base of the outputs is difficult to assess (e.g. many financial services) or for policy reasons (health care, education, culture).

- Tax legislation may also impose value added tax on businesses to secure effective taxation of final consumption. This might be the case when the business makes transactions that fall outside the scope of the tax (e.g. transactions without consideration) or the input tax relates to purchases that are not wholly used for furtherance of taxable business activity.

- Jurisdictions also provide legislation that disallows input tax recovery where explicit administrative obligations are not met (e.g. insufficient evidence to support input tax deduction).

2.5   Any such imposition of VAT on business should be clear and explicit within the legislative framework for the tax.

Guideline 2.2

Businesses in similar situations carrying out similar transactions should be subject to similar levels of taxation.

2.6   The tax should be neutral and equitable in similar circumstances. This is to ensure that the tax ultimately collected along a particular supply chain is proportional to the amount paid by the final consumer, whatever the nature of the supply, the structure of the distribution chain, the number of transactions or economic operators involved and the technical means used.

Guideline 2.3

VAT rules should be framed in such a way that they are not the primary influence on business decisions.

2.7   It is recognised that there are, in fact, a number of factors that can influence business decisions, including financial, commercial, social, environmental and legal factors. Whilst VAT is also a factor that is likely to be considered, it should not be the primary driver for business decisions. For example, VAT rules or policies should not induce businesses to adopt specific legal forms under which they operate (e.g. whether in a subsidiary or a branch structure).

2.8   VAT considerations include the amount of tax ultimately paid to tax administrations, the compliance burdens related to the collection, payment or refund of the tax such as filing of tax returns, maintaining adequate book-keeping and the financial costs related to the cash-flow impact of the VAT system.

2.9   In addition, to support the neutrality principle, the VAT rules should be accessible, clear and consistent.

C. Neutrality in international trade

C.1. Taxation principles

2.10   The general principles underpinning neutrality described above and the Guidelines that flow from them apply equally to domestic and international trade. One question is whether there are any additional considerations that need to be taken into account in the international context.

2.11   It is particularly important that the application of the rules for international supplies does not produce a tax advantage when compared with comparable domestic transactions. This includes the level at which taxation is applied, the costs of collection and administration and the corresponding burdens placed on businesses and tax administrations.

Guideline 2.4

With respect to the level of taxation, foreign businesses should not be disadvantaged or advantaged compared to domestic businesses in the jurisdiction where the tax may be due or paid.

2.12   VAT systems are designed to apply in a fair and even-handed way to ensure there is no unfair competitive advantage afforded to domestic or foreign businesses that may otherwise distort international trade and limit consumer choice. This is achieved by the application of the destination principle, under which exports are free of VAT and imports are taxed on the same basis and at the same rate as domestic supplies. The destination principle ensures that the net tax burden on imports is equal to the net tax burden on the same supplies in the domestic market. In addition, it also ensures that the amount of tax refunded or credited in the case of exports is equal to the amount of tax that has been levied.

2.13   The embedded features of the VAT system, when combined with the destination principle should ensure the same neutrality for international trade. However, there are in practice a number of cases where the standard rules will not apply and foreign businesses will incur VAT in a jurisdiction where they are neither established nor registered. Normally, the right of deduction of VAT is exercised by reducing the net tax payable. However, when foreign businesses incur VAT on business expenditures in a jurisdiction where they are not registered (or required to be registered) for VAT, this process cannot be applied.

2.14   The application of the principle that VAT should be neutral and equitable in similar circumstances to international trade implies that the VAT system should not encourage or discourage businesses from investing in or undertaking activities in a specific country. Such business decisions should be made on the basis of market and other non-tax considerations. This means that legislation in place in the country where VAT is incurred by foreign businesses should not discriminate against them nor favour them as regards the imposition of tax and their right of deduction or recovery of VAT compared to domestic businesses. Some tax administrations make reference to reciprocity when setting norms for refunds or equivalent mechanisms.

Guideline 2.5

To ensure foreign businesses do not incur irrecoverable VAT, jurisdictions may choose from a number of approaches.

2.15   The basic principles of VAT are broadly the same across jurisdictions that impose VAT, in that they aim to tax consumption in the jurisdiction where it occurs. However, differences exist between them as to the means used to achieve this objective. These differences may have many causes, including local history and traditions and the need to achieve specific policy objectives. These differences include the different approaches jurisdictions take to ensure neutrality of taxation in respect of foreign businesses.

2.16   The approaches adopted by jurisdictions to ensure the principle that foreign businesses should not incur irrecoverable VAT include:

● the operation of a system of applying for direct refunds of local VAT incurred

● making supplies free of VAT

● enabling refunds through local VAT registration

● shifting the responsibility on to locally registered suppliers/customers, and

● granting purchase exemption certificates.

2.17   Some jurisdictions may adopt only one approach, but others use a combination of different approaches.

2.18   Each approach seeks to ensure that foreign businesses do not incur irrecoverable VAT. It is likely that each approach will have its merits in particular circumstances, as each seeks to strike a balance between the relative compliance costs for businesses (both local supplier and foreign customer), on the one hand and administrative costs and the risks of tax evasion and avoidance for the tax authorities, on the other hand. The key is to find a reasonable balance between the two, while ensuring that, to the greatest extent possible, foreign businesses do not incur irrecoverable VAT, except where explicitly provided for in legislation on a basis that does not allow unjustified discrimination.[8] As a result, none of the approaches is to be preferred as a general rule.

C.2. Administration and compliance

2.19   As with many other taxes, VAT imposes compliance costs and burdens on businesses and administrative costs and burdens on the tax authorities. Examples of costs associated with VAT compliance include costs related to administration (e.g. employees and the costs of collection and recovery), infrastructure (e.g. costs associated with establishing systems and processes, including making software changes) and finance (e.g. cash-flow costs and the costs of bank guarantees).

2.20   Paragraph 2.7 outlines the principle that VAT considerations should not be the primary driver for business decisions. Paragraph 2.8 recognises that VAT considerations go beyond the amount of tax ultimately paid to tax administrations and include the associated costs.

2.21   The principle that businesses should not incur irrecoverable VAT (except in the circumstances contemplated by paragraph 2.4) does not mean that compliance costs and burdens should not be borne by businesses. Similarly, tax administrations will incur costs and burdens in managing VAT systems, including the underlying procedures and policies. Although some form of VAT refund or relief mechanism should generally be available to foreign businesses, the availability and scope of such systems or mechanisms may take into account the related burdens of administration, collection and enforcement. For example, the tax administration should not be expected to incur disproportionate costs or burdens when dealing with foreign businesses, such as might be the case when dealing with low value or *de minimis* claims.

Guideline 2.6

Where specific administrative requirements for foreign businesses are deemed necessary, they should not create a disproportionate or inappropriate compliance burden for the businesses.

---

8.   Article 24 of the OECD Model Tax Convention on Income and on Capital and its commentary provide principles, examples and reflections on the concept of non-discrimination.

2.22   It may be appropriate for tax administrations to impose specific compliance requirements on different categories of businesses. This may apply, for example, to small enterprises and enterprises in specific sectors or to foreign businesses. Indeed, dealing with foreign businesses with no "legal" presence in a jurisdiction inevitably brings an element of risk for tax administrations and they may need to take appropriate measures to protect against evasion and avoidance. However, tax administrations are encouraged to take full advantage of those available instruments that support exchange of information and mutual assistance in debt recovery (e.g. the *Multilateral Convention on Mutual Administrative Assistance in Tax Matters*).

2.23   Tax administrations should also seek to balance these appropriate measures with the need to prevent unjustified discrimination. Specific rules applicable to foreign businesses should not result in a disguised form of discrimination. It is also important that such specific requirements are clear, consistent and accessible to foreign businesses.

D. Applying the VAT neutrality principles in the context of cross-border trade: Commentary on the Guidelines on neutrality

2.24   The aim of this Commentary is to provide guidance for the implementation of the Guidelines on neutrality in practice.

2.25   For each Guideline, there is a specific Commentary in Section D.4 below that is intended to illustrate or provide further details on, but not change, its provisions.

D.1. Principles of good tax administration

2.26   The Guidelines on neutrality are not intended to interfere with the sovereignty of jurisdictions to apply tax rules for limiting the right to deduct input VAT, to exempt particular activities from VAT, or to establish specific administrative requirements for dealing with different categories of business (including foreign businesses). However, in order to ensure neutrality, jurisdictions are encouraged to apply the *General Administrative Principles* approved in 2001 by the OECD Forum on Tax Administration,[9] which are reproduced in Box 2.1 below.

---

9.   OECD (2001), Principles of Good Tax Administration – Practice Note, OECD, Paris, *www.oecd.org/tax/administration/1907918.pdf*.

Box 2.1. **Guidance – Relations with Taxpayers**

Revenue authorities are encouraged to:

1. apply tax laws in a fair, reliable and transparent manner

2. outline and communicate to taxpayers their rights and obligations as well as the available complaint procedures and redress mechanisms

3. consistently deliver quality information and treat inquiries, requests and appeals from taxpayers in an accurate and timely fashion

4. provide an accessible and dependable information service on taxpayers rights and obligations with respect to the law

5. ensure that compliance costs are kept at the minimum level necessary to achieve compliance with the tax laws

6. where appropriate, give taxpayers opportunities to comment on changes to administrative policies and procedures

7. use taxpayer information only to the extent permitted by law

8. develop and maintain good working relationships with client groups and the wider community.

D.2. Reciprocity

2.27   According to the Guidelines on neutrality, foreign businesses should not be disadvantaged or advantaged compared to domestic businesses. This means that foreign businesses should not incur irrecoverable VAT when this would constitute an unjustified discrimination compared to domestic businesses. A number of approaches can be used for this purpose such as direct refunds to foreign businesses, refunds through a domestic registration procedure or making supplies VAT free.

2.28   Some jurisdictions require that the granting of refunds to foreign businesses be conditional upon similar relief being granted by the jurisdiction of the foreign business claimant. These requirements for reciprocity generally take two forms: a formal bilateral agreement between jurisdictions or a unilateral decision to recognise jurisdictions considered as having (or not having) appropriate features in their legislation.[10]

2.29   The Guidelines take no position on the desirability of jurisdictions adopting reciprocity requirements. However, insofar as jurisdictions choose to

---

10. Reciprocity is currently applied by some countries that operate "direct refund mechanisms" (i.e. refunds through a stand-alone procedure, rather than through a local registration). However, it is possible that a reciprocity requirement is applied by jurisdictions using other means of ensuring neutrality, in which case the same guidance in this commentary also applies.

adopt such requirements, they should do so in a manner that minimises their impact on neutrality.

2.30   It is important to consider the scope of the reciprocity requirements. Indeed, in the context of the Guidelines, a reciprocal mechanism would not be required from a jurisdiction that does not have a VAT system, as defined for purposes of these Guidelines.[11] Jurisdictions are encouraged to treat other jurisdictions' mechanisms as satisfying reciprocity requirements if they are designed to ensure VAT-neutral treatment for foreign businesses and achieve a substantially equivalent treatment. A substantially equivalent treatment might, for example, result from a mixture of VAT free supplies and local registration mechanisms, as much as from the application of a direct refund approach.[12]

D.3. Groups of countries

2.31   Based on the principle set out in the *Guidelines on Consumption Taxation of Cross-Border Services and Intangible Property in the Context of E-commerce* and in accordance with the Ottawa Taxation Framework Conditions, a group of countries bound by a common legal framework for their VAT system may apply specific measures to transactions between those countries.[13] If this gives rise to a difference of treatment between member countries of such a group and non-member countries, but the treatment of non-member countries would not otherwise be inconsistent with the Guidelines on neutrality, the difference should not be regarded as being inconsistent with these Guidelines.

D.4. Commentary on the Guidelines

D.4.1. Commentary on Guideline 2.1

The burden of value added taxes themselves should not lie on taxable businesses except where explicitly provided for in legislation.

2.32   VAT normally flows through businesses so that the final consumer, not the business, bears the burden of the tax. In domestic trade, VAT neutrality is achieved by the staged payment system: each business pays VAT to its suppliers on its inputs and receives VAT from its customers on its outputs. Input VAT incurred by each business is offset against output VAT so that the amount of tax to be remitted to tax authorities by each business is the net amount or balance of those two. In some cases, the result of the offset gives rise to a refund

---

11. See Chapter 1. Where a jurisdiction operates a hybrid system, the part of the system that is not a VAT would not be considered.
12. Germany has expressed a reservation on this paragraph.
13. OECD (2001), *Taxation and Electronic Commerce – Implementing the Ottawa Taxation Framework Conditions*, OECD, Paris, footnote 6, page 45.

due by the tax authorities to the business. Examples include businesses that incur more tax on their inputs than is due on their outputs (such as exporters, as their output is free of VAT under the destination principle) and businesses whose purchases are larger than their sales in the same period (such as with new or developing businesses or seasonal businesses).

2.33   In cross-border trade, the neutrality of the tax is achieved by the application of the destination principle. According to this principle, exports are not subject to tax (free of VAT) and imports are taxed on the same basis and at the same rates as domestic supplies. This implies that the total tax paid in relation to a supply is ultimately determined by the rules applicable in the jurisdiction of its consumption and therefore all revenue accrues to the jurisdiction where the supply to the final customer occurs. In some instances, however, foreign businesses may incur VAT in jurisdictions where they cannot recover the input tax by way of deduction through the same procedures as domestic businesses. As in the case of domestic businesses, foreign businesses should not bear the burden of the tax itself, except where provided for in legislation.

2.34   Although the burden of VAT should not fall on businesses, Guideline 2.1 recognises that jurisdictions may legitimately place a VAT burden on them when this is specifically set out in legislation. Guideline 2.1 and this corresponding Commentary do not seek to make any judgement about the circumstances in which it may or may not be appropriate to place a VAT burden on businesses. They simply recognise that jurisdictions may do so.

2.35   Guideline 2.1 is not intended to interfere with the sovereignty of jurisdictions to apply rules for limiting or blocking the right to deduct input VAT. However, in order to ensure neutrality, in applying such rules, tax administrations are encouraged to apply the principles of good tax administration as set out in Box 2.1.

2.36   When jurisdictions do impose a VAT burden on businesses, legislation that so provides should be, in accordance with Box 2.1, clear and transparent and should keep compliance costs to a minimum.

2.37   The reference to explicit provisions in the legislation in Guideline 2.1 is not limited to provisions of the law itself but also includes explicit provisions made under the law, such as in regulations or as a result of the exercise of administrative powers granted by the legislation. Decisions of courts of the relevant jurisdiction should also be taken into consideration.

2.38   When a tax burden is placed on businesses, an explicit provision for such a burden in legislation does not suffice to make it consistent with the Guidelines on neutrality. It simply means that Guideline 2.1 is met. If the legislation in question does not meet the other five Guidelines on neutrality, or is inconsistent with the Guidelines as a whole, such legislation cannot be seen as meeting the neutrality principles.

D.4.2. Commentary on Guideline 2.2

Businesses in similar situations carrying out similar transactions should be subject to similar levels of taxation.

2.39   The main goal of Guideline 2.2 is to ensure that "similar levels of taxation" are achieved. However, this goal is recognised only with respect to "businesses in similar situations" that are carrying out "similar transactions". If either one of these conditions is not satisfied, Guideline 2.2 has no application. Accordingly, in explaining the meaning of the Guideline, it is essential to define the concepts of "similar levels of taxation", "businesses in similar situations" and "similar transactions."

D.4.2.1. Similar levels of taxation

2.40   In the context of the Guidelines on neutrality, when determining whether a "similar level of taxation" has been achieved, the final tax burden needs to be considered, taking into account all available refunds and credits. Businesses with full right to deduct input tax should not bear any tax burden, whether the services and intangibles they use to make their onward supplies are acquired abroad or in the domestic market. When a business without full right to deduct input tax incurs VAT in different jurisdictions, it should bear the burden of the VAT only once on each input. If such a business were to incur irrecoverable tax in two or more jurisdictions on the same input, it would not bear a "similar level of taxation" compared to another business without full right to deduct input tax that acquired its inputs solely within the domestic market.

2.41   Guideline 2.2 applies only to the VAT burden directly incurred by businesses. Guideline 2.2 does not cover situations where businesses indirectly incur a positive level of taxation, for example, where they acquire exempt services for which the supplier did not have a right to deduct its own input tax. In this case, the price paid by the business customer to its supplier may include embedded VAT that the supplier is unable to recover.

D.4.2.2. Businesses in similar situations

2.42   Determining whether businesses are in "similar situations" should be assessed with respect to their right of deduction, determined by the extent to which their inputs are used to support taxable activities (which give rise to the right to deduct the related input tax). A business that is acquiring services to support its taxable activities would not be in a "similar situation" to a business acquiring services to support its exempt activities or to one that acquires services predominantly for the personal use of its owners. A "similar situation" should not be restricted to a comparison of similar industries.

2.43   The following are examples of businesses in similar situations, based on their right of deduction:

- A consulting company that has a full right to deduct input tax in comparison to an airline company with a full right to deduct input tax.
- A bank that normally has a limited right to deduct input tax in comparison to an insurance company that has a limited right to deduct input tax.
- A consulting company that has a full right to deduct input tax in comparison to a bank that also has a full right to deduct input tax (e.g. because its outputs are fully taxed or zero-rated).
- A business that normally has a limited right to deduct input tax, which acquires services for the private use of its owners, in comparison to a business that normally has a full right to deduct input tax and has acquired services for the private use of its owners.

2.44   The following are examples of businesses in dissimilar situations:

- A consulting company that has a full right to deduct input tax in comparison to a bank that has a limited right to deduct input tax.
- A financial institution that has a full right of deduction (e.g. because its outputs are fully taxed or zero-rated) in comparison to a financial institution that has a limited right of deduction (e.g. because it provides exempt financial services to domestic customers).
- A business that normally has a full right to deduct input tax and acquires services for the private use of its owners, in comparison to a business that has a full right to deduct input tax that acquires services for use in its taxable activities.

D.4.2.3. Similar transactions

2.45   The determination of "similar transactions" for businesses "in similar situations" purchasing services or intangibles should focus on the characterisation of the particular services or intangibles being supplied. Once the characterisation has been determined, the way the supply was made, the person from whom it was acquired within the supply chain, or the terms under which the services or intangibles were acquired are not relevant.

2.46   The characterisation of a supply may not be consistent across jurisdictions. For example some jurisdictions may apply a specific tax treatment to a number of well-defined services or intangibles while other jurisdictions have a single characterisation of services and then a single tax treatment for their supply. For that reason it is important to consider the characterisation of the supply under the rules in the jurisdiction in which businesses are being compared.

D.4.2.4. Summary

2.47   To summarise, the following factors are to be considered in determining when tax burdens, situations and transactions, respectively, are similar.

- Businesses incur "similar levels of taxation" when they do not incur a tax burden, or, if they do directly incur irrecoverable VAT, when that tax burden is incurred only once on the same supply, which would also be the case for a business in a similar situation.

- Businesses are in "similar situations" based on their use of the services or intangibles and their related right to deduct input tax (i.e. the supply is used to further taxable activities, exempt activities or is for personal use – which will determine the right to deduct input tax).

- Businesses are carrying out "similar transactions" based on the characterisation of the supply under the rules in the jurisdiction in which the businesses are being compared.

D.4.3. Commentary on Guideline 2.3

VAT rules should be framed in such a way that they are not the primary influence on business decisions.

2.48   Inconsistency with Guideline 2.3 relating to the impact of VAT on business decisions is likely to reflect an inconsistency with one of the other Guidelines. Where this is the case, businesses may try to restructure their supply chain or operations to achieve the neutrality that does not otherwise exist. In the context of Guideline 2.3, VAT considerations include a combination of the amount of tax ultimately paid to tax administrations, the associated compliance burdens, and the financial costs related to the cash-flow impact of the VAT system.

2.49   For example, in situations where foreign businesses are advantaged compared to domestic businesses in respect of the level of taxation (which is inconsistent with Guideline 2.4), a foreign business may change the decision it would otherwise make primarily in order to take advantage of this treatment. Thus, a business may decide to operate from offshore rather than in the domestic jurisdiction.

2.50   When evaluating a jurisdiction where a domestic business can fully recover local VAT, a foreign business that would not be eligible for VAT recovery, refund, or relief may decide, based primarily on the VAT burden, that it will not undertake activities (sales, purchases, or related activities such as production or support services) in that jurisdiction or that it will restructure the supply chain to achieve the neutrality that does not otherwise exist.

2.51   In order to assess the consistency of the VAT rules with Guideline 2.3, the business decisions that are relevant would be those relating to cross-border operations, which may be affected by the VAT legislation, such as:

- whether a business will decide to operate in a jurisdiction
- whether a business will sell to customers in a jurisdiction
- whether a business will make purchases from a vendor located in a jurisdiction
- whether a business will outsource activities such as production, manufacturing or other support services to be carried out in a jurisdiction, and
- how a business will structure its supply chain or make use of intermediaries.

2.52   By contrast, business decisions that are not relevant would be those relating to the domestic operations, such as:

- decisions not to purchase or sell items on which there is a block on input tax credits (e.g. in some jurisdictions there is a difference between leased and purchased items)
- altering products or services to take advantage of a different tax status (e.g. taxable at a positive rate, exempt, or zero-rated), and
- taking advantage of simplified methods of calculating taxes due, which may be available to smaller suppliers.

D.4.4. Commentary on Guideline 2.4

With respect to the level of taxation, foreign businesses should not be disadvantaged or advantaged compared to domestic businesses in the jurisdiction where the tax may be due or paid.

2.53   Guideline 2.2 deals with equity of treatment for businesses in similar situations carrying out similar transactions. Guideline 2.4 deals with equity of treatment for foreign businesses relative to domestic businesses in a jurisdiction where foreign businesses may otherwise bear a VAT burden that would not apply to domestic businesses or vice-versa.

2.54   In the context of the Guidelines and with respect to the level of VAT incurred, "foreign businesses should not be disadvantaged or advantaged compared to domestic businesses in the jurisdiction where the tax may be due or paid" should be understood to mean that:

- there should not be any discriminatory application of the rules simply because a business is foreign;
- foreign businesses should not end up having a tax advantage compared to domestic businesses in terms of their final tax burden, and
- if Guideline 2.4 is followed, VAT should not distort competition between foreign and domestic businesses.[14]

2.55   This Guideline deals with the ultimate application of VAT on businesses. Foreign businesses should not be subject to irrecoverable VAT compared to domestic businesses, however that outcome is achieved, e.g. through application of zero-rate rules, refund mechanisms, *etc*. Nor would the creation of a tax advantage, in terms of the final tax burden, for foreign businesses compared to domestic businesses acting in similar circumstances be consistent with this Guideline. Guideline 2.4 is met, when legislation provides a refund or other form of relief mechanism to foreign businesses, in such a way that they are not advantaged or disadvantaged compared to domestic businesses.

D.4.5. *Commentary on Guideline 2.5*

To ensure foreign businesses do not incur irrecoverable VAT, jurisdictions may choose from a number of approaches

2.56   A range of approaches could be used to ensure that foreign businesses do not incur irrecoverable VAT. These include (but are not limited to):

● making supplies free of VAT

● allowing foreign businesses to obtain a refund through a specific regime

● allowing foreign businesses to obtain a refund through local VAT registration

● shifting the responsibility to locally registered suppliers/customers,[15] and

● granting purchase exemption certificates.[16]

2.57   Each approach seeks to ensure that foreign businesses do not incur irrecoverable VAT. None of the approaches is to be preferred over the others. It is likely that each approach will have its merits in particular circumstances, as each seeks to strike a balance between the relative compliance costs for businesses (both local supplier and foreign customer), on the one hand, and administrative costs and the risks of tax evasion and avoidance for the tax authorities, on the other. Jurisdictions may prefer to apply a mix of different approaches depending on the nature of the supplies involved. For example, for some supplies, making supplies VAT free may be preferred to direct refunds or registration because it removes the compliance costs for businesses of having

---

14. Germany has expressed a reservation on this paragraph.
15. Some countries provide for a shift in responsibilities to allow either a) a purchaser to claim input tax that was charged to a non-resident vendor who is not registered for local VAT, or b) services to be provided on a VAT free basis to a non-resident who is not registered, even though the services may closely relate to property that is located in the local country, when the property to which the services relate will subsequently be delivered to a registrant in the local country.
16. Some countries allow a non-resident purchaser who may or may not be registered locally to provide a purchase exemption certificate to allow the supplier to make a supply on a VAT free basis. The supplier would be responsible for retaining a copy of the purchase exemption certificate on file to substantiate why tax was not charged to the non-resident.

to claim the VAT back. For other supplies, a refund or registration system may be preferred because of the difficulty faced by the supplier in determining the status and location of the customer.

2.58   Jurisdictions will seek to protect their tax bases from evasion and avoidance and to use all reasonable methods to achieve this objective. However, cost effectiveness is important to any mechanism for achieving neutrality, including any refund and similar schemes. Measures taken by a jurisdiction to protect its tax base may therefore need to be balanced against the objective of keeping compliance and administrative costs as low as possible.

2.59   For example, a direct refund system that applies a *de minimis* threshold before refund applications are accepted would meet the neutrality objective provided that the threshold is reasonable and reflects the balance between the administrative costs of processing the refund and the amount of VAT involved. On the other hand, a registration system that does not allow refunds unless taxable supplies are made in the local jurisdiction by the non-resident business may not adequately meet the neutrality objective.

D.4.6. *Commentary on Guideline 2.6*

Where specific administrative requirements for foreign businesses are deemed necessary, they should not create a disproportionate or inappropriate compliance burden for the businesses.

2.60   Domestic businesses and foreign businesses are in different situations in relation to the tax administration. Domestic businesses will generally have a fixed place of business from which the business is operated, local employees and contact persons, a local bank, local links to the tax authorities and various forms of identification/registration through bodies such as the local Chamber of Commerce and Trade Registry. On the other hand, foreign businesses are less likely to have a legal presence, local staff or links with the local community.

2.61   This lack of presence and history in a jurisdiction inevitably brings an element of risk for tax administrations, for which appropriate measures may need to be taken to protect against evasion and avoidance. Specific compliance requirements may therefore be needed if the standard requirements applicable to domestic businesses do not provide adequate protection for jurisdictions. Tax administrations are also encouraged to take full advantage of available instruments that support exchange of information and mutual assistance in the assessment and collection of taxes (e.g. the *Multilateral Convention on Mutual Administrative Assistance in Tax Matters*).

2.62   In addition, where jurisdictions operate a relief mechanism specifically aimed at foreign businesses, they may also have specific rules and requirements for that mechanism.

2.63   The Guidelines on neutrality recognise that the administrative requirements for domestic and foreign businesses may not be identical. However, if jurisdictions choose to adopt specific rules and requirements for foreign businesses, they should do so in a manner that minimises their impact on neutrality.

2.64   In essence, where there is an element of additional compliance burden associated with doing business in a foreign jurisdiction, the burden created by the specific administrative requirements should not be disproportionate or inappropriate.

2.65   A requirement or combination of requirements may be disproportionate or inappropriate if it is out of proportion to the situation to which it relates or if it does not achieve a relevant purpose when assessed and measured against the objective it is aiming to achieve. In other words, in the context of the Guidelines, such a requirement or combination of requirements should not be disproportionate or inappropriate to any additional risk involved in dealing with a foreign business.

2.66   An appropriate balance is needed between the perceived benefits of a specific requirement or combination of requirements and the need to prevent unjustified discrimination. In other words, specific rules or practices (e.g. audits, time taken to provide a refund) applicable to foreign businesses should not result in a disguised form of discrimination and should also meet the guiding principles set out in Box 2.1.

2.67   For example, if a tax administration requires a bank guarantee, the amount and duration should not be disproportionate to the amount of the refund claimed. Similarly, when documentation is required to support a refund claim (possibly in the language of the country where the claim is lodged), it should be limited to the documents that are necessary to the assessment of the validity of the claim. In addition, the time taken to make a refund and the resulting cash-flow burden should be taken into account.

2.68   Tax administrations will also incur administrative costs in managing specific relief mechanisms aimed at foreign businesses (e.g. a refund mechanism). When they set up *de minimis* thresholds, these thresholds should not effectively prevent the use of the mechanism.

2.69   Whilst the concept of specific administrative requirements for foreign businesses is generally understood to mean additional and more complex requirements, this is not always the case. In some instances, tax administrations can set up a simplified compliance system specifically for foreign businesses. Examples include specific provisions for making supplies free of VAT, applicable to supplies to foreign businesses, as well as simplified registration and reporting procedures for foreign businesses.

2.70   Finally, specific administrative requirements or simplifications adopted by a group of countries that are bound by a common legal framework for their consumption tax systems may differ from those applicable to businesses from other countries. As expressed in paragraph 2.31 such a difference of treatment should not be regarded as being inconsistent with Guideline 2.6.

Chapter 3

Determining the place of taxation for cross-border supplies of services and intangibles

A. The destination principle

3.1   VAT neutrality in international trade is generally achieved through the implementation of the "destination principle". As explained in Chapter 1, the destination principle is designed to ensure that tax on cross-border supplies is ultimately levied only in the jurisdiction where the final consumption occurs, thereby maintaining neutrality within the VAT system as it applies to international trade. This principle is set out in Guideline 3.1.

Guideline 3.1

For consumption tax purposes internationally traded services and intangibles should be taxed according to the rules of the jurisdiction of consumption.

3.2   In order to apply the destination principle to internationally traded services and intangibles, VAT systems must have mechanisms for identifying the jurisdiction of consumption by connecting such supplies to the jurisdiction where the final consumption of the services or intangibles is expected to take place. VAT systems need place of taxation rules to implement the destination principle not only for business-to-consumer supplies, which involve final consumption, but also for business-to-business supplies, even though such supplies do not involve final consumption. Business-to-business supplies are taxed under the VAT's staged collection process, and, in this context, the place of taxation rules should facilitate the ultimate objective of the tax, which is to tax final consumption. These Guidelines set out the recommended approaches that reflect the destination principle for determining the place of taxation for business-to-consumer and business-to-business cross-border supplies of services and intangibles.

3.3   Place of taxation rules are needed for supplies of goods as well as for supplies of services and intangibles. Implementing the destination principle with respect to cross-border supplies of goods is facilitated by the existence of border controls or fiscal frontiers. Implementing the destination principle with respect to international trade in services and intangibles is more difficult, because the nature of services and intangibles is such that they cannot be subject to border controls in the same way as goods. The Guidelines in this

Chapter therefore concentrate on supplies of services and intangibles.[17] They set out recommended approaches that reflect the destination principle for determining the jurisdiction of taxation for international supplies of services and intangibles while ensuring that:

- international neutrality is maintained;
- compliance by businesses involved in these supplies is kept as simple as possible;
- clarity and certainty are provided for both business and tax administrations;
- the costs involved in complying with the tax and administering it are minimal, and
- barriers to evasion and avoidance are sufficiently robust.

3.4   This Chapter should not be read as requiring jurisdictions to literally incorporate the Guidelines on determining the place of taxation as legal rules in national legislation. These Guidelines seek to identify common objectives and suggest means for achieving them with a view to promoting a consistent implementation of the destination principle for determining the place of taxation for supplies of services and intangibles. It is recognised that a variety of models for structuring and designing place of taxation rules are operated by VAT systems around the world. Many systems operate on the basis of a categorisation approach, in which supplies are divided into categories with a place of taxation specified for each category. Other models favour an iterative approach, in which the principle underlying the place of taxation rule is described in more general terms and where a series of rules are applied consecutively to determine the appropriate place of taxation. These differences in legal drafting style are generally not absolute and elements of both approaches can be found in both models. The key common feature among the various VAT design models is that they generally aim to implement the destination principle, under which the place of taxation rules are intended to impose tax at the place of consumption. These Guidelines seek to ensure that these place of taxation rules are applied consistently by promoting an internationally accepted understanding of what is the place of taxation of internationally traded services and intangibles and by setting out consistent

---

17. For the purposes of these Guidelines, a supply of services or intangibles for VAT purposes takes place where one party does something for, or gives something (other than something tangible) to another party or refrains from doing something for another party, in exchange for consideration. It is recognised that a supply of services or intangibles in one country may in certain instances be regarded as a supply of goods (or some other category of supply) in another country. Where this is the case, and while these Guidelines deal only with supplies of services and intangibles, countries are encouraged to ensure that the rules for identifying the place of taxation of such supplies lead to a result that is consistent with these Guidelines.

and effective approaches for determining this place of taxation with a view to minimizing uncertainty, revenue risks, compliance costs and administrative burdens for tax authorities and businesses.

3.5   The approaches used by VAT systems to implement the destination principle for business-to-business supplies and the tax collection methods used for such supplies are often different from those used for business-to-consumer supplies. This distinction is attributable to the different objectives of taxing business-to-business and business-to-consumer supplies: taxation of business-to-consumer supplies involves the imposition of a final tax burden, while taxation of business-to-business supplies is merely a means of achieving the ultimate objective of the tax, which is to tax final consumption. Thus, the objective of place of taxation rules for business-to-business supplies is primarily to facilitate the imposition of a tax burden on the final consumer in the appropriate country while maintaining neutrality within the VAT system. The place of taxation rules for business-to-business supplies should therefore focus not only on where the business customer will use its purchases to create the goods, services or intangibles that final consumers will acquire, but also on facilitating the flow-through of the tax burden to the final consumer while maintaining neutrality within the VAT system. The overriding objective of place of taxation rules for business-to-consumer supplies, on the other hand, is to predict, subject to practical constraints, the place where the final consumer is likely to consume the services or intangibles supplied. In addition to the different objectives of the place of taxation rules for business-to-business and business-to-consumer supplies, VAT systems often employ different mechanisms to enforce and collect the tax for both categories of supplies. These different collection mechanisms often influence the design of place of taxation rules and of the compliance obligations for suppliers and customers involved in cross-border supplies. In light of these considerations, this Chapter presents separate Guidelines for determining the place of taxation for business-to-business supplies and for business-to-consumer supplies. This should not be interpreted as a recommendation to jurisdictions to develop separate rules or implement different mechanisms for each type of supply in their national legislation.

3.6   In theory, place of taxation rules should aim to identify the actual place of business use for business-to-business supplies (on the assumption that this best facilitates implementation of the destination principle) and the actual place of final consumption for business-to-consumer supplies. However, these Guidelines recognise that place of taxation rules are in practice rarely aimed at identifying where business use or final consumption actually takes place. This is a consequence of the fact that VAT must in principle be charged at or before the time when the object of the supply is made available for business use or final consumption. In most cases, at that time the supplier will not know or be able to ascertain where such business use or final consumption will actually occur. VAT systems therefore generally use proxies for the place of business use or final consumption to determine the jurisdiction of taxation, based on features of the supply that are known or knowable at the time that the tax treatment of the supply must be determined. The Guidelines in this Chapter identify such proxies for determining the place of taxation of supplies of services and intangibles, both for business-to-business supplies and for business-to-consumer supplies.

3.7   For the purposes of these Guidelines business-to-business supplies are assumed to be supplies where both the supplier and the customer are recognised as businesses, and business-to-consumer supplies are assumed to be supplies where the customer is not recognised as a business. Such recognition may include the treatment for VAT purposes specifically or in national law more generally (notably in jurisdictions that have not implemented a VAT).

3.8   Jurisdictions that implement different approaches for determining the place of taxation and/or different collection mechanisms for business-to-business supplies and for business-to-consumer supplies are encouraged to provide clear practical guidance on how suppliers can establish the status of their customer (business or non-business). Jurisdictions may consider adopting a requirement for suppliers to provide a customer's VAT registration number, business tax identification number, or other such indicia (e.g. information available in commercial registers) to establish their customer's status. Where a supplier, acting in good faith and having made reasonable efforts, is not able to obtain the appropriate documentation to establish the status of its customer, this could lead to a presumption that this is a non-business customer in which case the rules for business-to-consumer supplies would apply. To facilitate suppliers' identification and verification of their customers' status, jurisdictions are encouraged to consider implementing an easy-to-use process that would allow suppliers to verify the validity of their customers' VAT registration or tax identification numbers. Where, in respect of some or all types of services, jurisdictions do not distinguish between business-to-business and business-to-consumer supplies, such guidance might not be necessary.

B. Business-to-business supplies – The general rule

B.1. Defining the general rule

> **Guideline 3.2**
>
> For the application of Guideline 3.1, for business-to-business supplies, the jurisdiction in which the customer is located has the taxing rights over internationally traded services or intangibles.

3.9   By and large, when a business buys in services or intangibles from another jurisdiction, it does so for the purposes of its business operations. As such, the jurisdiction of the customer's location can stand as the appropriate proxy for the jurisdiction of business use, as it achieves the objective of neutrality by implementing the destination principle. This is the jurisdiction where the customer has located its permanent business presence.

3.10   This proxy is referred to in these Guidelines as the general rule for business-to-business supplies, as distinguished from specific rules that are covered by Guidelines 3.7 and 3.8. According to this general rule, the jurisdiction where the customer is located has the taxing rights over services or intangibles supplied across international borders. The supplier makes the supply free of VAT in its jurisdiction but retains the right to full input tax credit (subject to clearly legislated exceptions in that jurisdiction) on inputs related to making such international supplies. Only in exceptional and clearly specified circumstances should the place of taxation vary from this general rule.[18]

3.11   This section and the following sections provide further guidance on how the jurisdiction of a customer's location can be determined.

Guideline 3.3

For the application of Guideline 3.2, the identity of the customer is normally determined by reference to the business agreement.

3.12   Under Guideline 3.3, the identity of the customer is "normally determined by reference to the business agreement" as it is expected that business agreements reflect the underlying supply. The business agreement will assist the supplier, the customer and tax administrations in identifying the nature of the supply and the identity of the parties to the supply. When supplies are made between separate legal entities with only a single location, the location of the customer also will be known once the identity of the customer is determined.[19] It is appropriate to first describe "business agreement" for the purposes of these Guidelines and explain how tax administrations and businesses may approach the determination of the business agreement.

---

18. See Guideline 3.7.

19. When a supply is made to a legal entity that has establishments in more than one jurisdiction (a "multiple location entity", "MLE"), an additional analysis is required to determine which of the jurisdictions where this MLE has establishments has taxing rights over the service or intangible acquired by the MLE. See Section B.3 below.

> ### Box 3.1. **Business Agreement**
>
> Business agreements consist of the elements that identify the parties to a supply and the rights and obligations with respect to that supply.[20] They are generally based on mutual understanding.[21]

3.13   The term "business agreement" has been adopted for the purpose of these Guidelines because it is a general concept, rather than a term with a technical meaning, and it is not specific to any individual jurisdiction. In particular, it is not restricted to a contract (whether written or in some other format) and is therefore wide in its application, as explained below.

3.14   In order to determine the place of taxation under the general rule, it is necessary to demonstrate the nature of the supply as well as the identity of the supplier and the customer.

3.15   In many cases, particularly those involving significant sums of money or complex matters beyond a straightforward supply, it is likely that the parties to a business agreement will draw up legally enforceable contracts. These contracts will normally specify the parties to the business agreement and set out their respective rights and obligations. However, contracts in themselves should not be seen as the only relevant elements of a business agreement.

3.16   Other relevant elements of the business agreement come in many forms and include, for example, general correspondence, purchase orders, invoices, payment instruments and receipts. Legislation and business practices in jurisdictions invariably differ and generally not for tax reasons. They may differ with respect to national laws concerning contract issues and other commercial requirements. They may also differ between different industry sectors. It is, therefore, neither possible nor desirable to draw up a prescriptive or exhaustive list of items that must be present in a business agreement. Rather, these Guidelines suggest sources of information that would help both tax administrations and business.

3.17   A business agreement need not be confined to written material. In certain sectors, relevant elements may be found in the form of audio recordings of telephone conversations leading to conclusions of agreements to supply or receive services and/or intangibles. Relevant elements of a business

---

20. Agreements that do not lead to supplies for tax purposes are not regarded on their own as "business agreements" for the purposes of these Guidelines.
21. It is recognised, however, that on occasion supplies may occur without a mutual understanding, e.g. a court order that imposes obligations on one or more parties. In such cases the "imposed" agreement should nevertheless be considered as a "business agreement".

agreement may also be found in electronic form such as e-mails and on-line ordering records, payment and similar material and formats that are likely to emerge as new technologies develop.

3.18   It is recognised that business agreements are often not concluded in isolation. Consequently other agreements, including those not regarded as business agreements (e.g. agreements that do not involve a supply[22]), may provide the context of the supplies made under a particular business agreement. These other agreements may therefore form a part of the relevant elements of that business agreement.

3.19   In the light of the previous paragraphs, the business agreement in force at the time the supply is made is the agreement that governs the implementation of the general rule.

3.20   To ease burdens in practice for both tax administrations and business, it is recommended that jurisdictions take into account the application of Guidelines 3.2 and 3.3 in a way that is consistent with the previous paragraphs. Wherever possible, tax administrations are encouraged to communicate these approaches and relevant national laws as clearly and as widely as possible.

B.2. Applying the general rule – Supply of a service or intangible to a legal entity with single location ("single location entity" – "SLE")

3.21   In principle, applying the general rule for business-to-business supplies to legal entities[23] with a single location ("single location entities" – "SLEs") is relatively straightforward. The Commentary under Section B.4 provides further practical guidance.

B.3. Applying the general rule – Supply of a service or intangible to a legal entity with multiple locations ("multiple location entity" – "MLE")

3.22   When a supply is made to a legal entity that has establishments[24] in more than one jurisdiction (a "multiple location entity", "MLE"), an analysis

---

22. An illustration of this is the Centralised Purchasing Agreement in Example 3 and the Framework Agreement in Examples 4 and 5 in Annex I to this Chapter.
23. Legal entities can include natural persons and non-commercial institutions such as governments, non-profit organisations and other institutions. The key point is that such entities, or certain of their activities, are recognised as "businesses" in national law. Such recognition may include the treatment for VAT purposes specifically or in national law more generally (notably in jurisdictions that have not implemented a VAT). See also paragraph 3.7.
24. For the purpose of these Guidelines, it is assumed that an establishment comprises a fixed place of business with a sufficient level of infrastructure in terms of people, systems and assets to be able to receive and/or make supplies. Registration for VAT purposes by itself does not constitute an establishment for the purposes of these Guidelines. Countries are encouraged to publicise what constitutes an "establishment" under their domestic VAT legislation.

is required to determine which of the jurisdictions where this MLE has establishments has taxing rights over the service or intangible acquired by the MLE.

3.23   In such a case, jurisdictions are encouraged to apply an approach that would ensure that taxation accrues to the jurisdiction where the customer's establishment using the service or intangible is located.

Guideline 3.4

For the application of Guideline 3.2, when the customer has establishments in more than one jurisdiction, the taxing rights accrue to the jurisdiction(s) where the establishment(s) using the service or intangible is (are) located.

3.24   "Use of a service or intangible"[25] in this context refers to the use of a service or intangible by a business for the purpose of its business operations. It is irrelevant whether this use is immediate, continuous, directly linked to an output transaction or supports the business operations in general.

3.25   A number of possible approaches are currently adopted by jurisdictions to identify which customer's establishment is regarded as using a service or intangible and where this establishment is located. The following broad categories of approaches can be distinguished:

● Direct use approach, which focuses directly on the establishment that uses the service or intangible.

● Direct delivery approach, which focuses on the establishment to which the service or intangible is delivered.

● Recharge method, which focuses on the establishment that uses the service or intangible as determined on the basis of internal recharge arrangements within the MLE, made in accordance with corporate tax, accounting or other regulatory requirements.

3.26   Each of the approaches described above seeks to ensure that taxation of the supply of a service or intangible to a MLE accrues to the jurisdiction where the customer's establishment that is regarded as using the service or intangibles is located. It is likely that each of these approaches will

---

25. "Use of a service or intangible" in this context differs from the concept of "use and enjoyment" existing in some national laws, which can refer to actual use by a customer in a jurisdiction irrespective of the presence of any customer establishment. See also Section D. on the use of specific rules for determining the place of taxation.

have its merits in particular circumstances. The principle behind any approach should be to achieve a sound balance between the interests of business (both suppliers and customers) and tax administrations.

B.3.1. Direct use

3.27   Under this approach, taxing rights for the supply of a service or intangible to a MLE are directly allocated to the jurisdiction of the customer's establishment that is regarded as using this service or intangible.

3.28   This approach may be particularly effective in circumstances where there is obvious use by an establishment of the customer MLE. It is then relatively straightforward for the supplier and customer to ensure that this is reflected properly in the business agreement. In these circumstances, both the supplier and the customer would have the necessary information to support a proper tax treatment at the time of the supply and the business agreement would provide an appropriate audit trail to the tax authorities.

3.29   This approach may be more difficult in circumstances where the supplier does not know, and perhaps cannot know, which customer establishment uses the supply or in circumstances where the actual use is not known with certainty at the time of the business agreement. This approach also may not deal adequately with cases where the service or intangible is used by different establishments in different jurisdictions ("multiple use"). In such cases this approach may create considerable compliance difficulties for suppliers and customers and may affect the efficiency of tax administration and collection.

B.3.2. Direct delivery

3.30   Under this approach, taxing rights for the supply of a service or intangible to a MLE are directly allocated to the jurisdiction of the customer's establishment to which the supplier delivers the service or intangible.

3.31   The "direct delivery" approach may provide an effective solution for supplies of services or intangibles that are likely to be used at the location of the establishment to which they are delivered ("physically supplied", such as catering or on-the-spot training). In such cases both the supplier and customer are likely to know the location of the establishment of direct delivery at the time of the supply and are likely to reflect this in the business agreement. The supplier and the customer would therefore have the necessary information to support a proper tax treatment at the time of the supply and the business agreement would provide an appropriate audit trail to the tax authorities.

B.3.3. Recharge method

3.32   This approach requires MLEs to internally recharge the cost of an externally acquired service or intangible to their establishments that use this service or intangible, as supported by internal recharge arrangements. Under the recharge method, these internal recharges are used as a basis for allocating the taxing rights over the external service or intangible to the jurisdiction where the MLE's establishment using this service or intangible is located. Further information and guidance on this approach is to be found in the Commentary under Section B.5 below.

3.33   This approach may be useful in cases where a service or intangible supplied by an external supplier to a MLE is acquired by one establishment of this MLE for use wholly or partially by other establishments located in different jurisdictions ("multiple use"). It is common practice for multinational businesses to arrange for a wide scope of services, such as administrative, technical, financial and commercial services, to be acquired centrally to realise economies of scale. Typically, the cost of acquiring such a service or intangible is then initially borne by the establishment that has acquired the service or intangible and, in line with normal business practice, is subsequently recharged to the establishments using the service or intangible. The establishments are charged for their share of the service or intangible on the basis of the internal recharge arrangements, in accordance with corporate tax, accounting and other regulatory requirements.

3.34   It may be difficult, if not impossible, for a supplier in such a multiple-use scenario to know which establishments of a MLE will actually use the service or intangible supplied to this MLE and to ensure a correct VAT treatment in accordance with the location of these establishments of use (see paragraph 3.29 above). Even if the supplier knew where the service or intangible supplied to a MLE were used, it could be challenging, particularly in a multiple-use scenario, to implement and administer a system whereby the supplier's taxing decision depends on the location of the establishments of use.

3.355   The recharge method could offer an effective solution for identifying the place of taxation of the supply of a service or intangible to a MLE, particularly in multiple-use scenarios. Under this approach, the supplier would rely on the business agreement with the MLE to support the proper VAT treatment of the supply to the MLE. It would be for the customer MLE to ensure the correct VAT treatment of this service or intangible, based on the internal allocation of the cost to its establishments using this service or intangible. This would build on existing business processes and information that will generally already be available for accounting, tax or other regulatory purposes, and would therefore not create undue compliance burdens. These processes and information should also facilitate the production of appropriate and reliable audit trails for tax authorities.

3.36   Jurisdictions that consider implementing the recharge method may need to address a number of potentially complex aspects of this method. These include questions regarding the scope of this method, acceptable methods for the proper allocation of taxable amounts to the establishment(s) of use and the timing of the recharges, the impact of internal recharges on the right to deduct input VAT and questions about documentation requirements and the process to account for any tax due on internal recharges. Jurisdictions may also need to take account of tax administration concerns such as the additional number of transactions that may have to be audited due to the internal recharges. Jurisdictions that consider implementing this recharge method are encouraged to take these concerns into careful consideration and to provide clear guidance on the operation of this method. The Commentary under Section B.5 below looks at a number of these aspects in further detail.

B.3.4. Conclusion

3.37   Each of the approaches described above seeks to ensure that taxation of the supply of a service or intangible to a MLE accrues to the jurisdiction where the customer's establishment(s) using the service or intangible is (are) located. These Guidelines do not aim to set out which approach should be preferred or to rule out alternatives: each approach is likely to have specific merits in particular circumstances. These approaches are not mutually exclusive and could be combined according to the information that is available to the supplier and the customer. It is for jurisdictions to adopt the approach or approaches that they consider appropriate, taking into account their legal and administrative framework and practices.

3.38   Any approach should, in principle:

- seek to ensure that taxation of the supply of a service or intangible to a MLE accrues to the jurisdiction(s) where the customer's establishment(s) regarded as using the service or intangible is (are) located; and

- achieve a sound balance between the interests of business (both suppliers and customers) and tax administrations.

3.39   Jurisdictions are encouraged to seek the right balance between the objectives of protecting tax revenue and of keeping compliance and administrative costs as low as possible, while minimizing distortions of competition. Jurisdictions are also encouraged to provide clear, accessible and dependable information to increase certainty and to ensure the correct VAT treatment of the supply of a service or intangible to a MLE, both by the supplier and by the customer.

3.40   The key objective of these Guidelines is to help reduce uncertainty and risks of double taxation and unintended non-taxation resulting from inconsistencies in the application of VAT to international trade. Jurisdictions are therefore encouraged to adopt an approach that minimises the potential for double taxation or unintended non-taxation. The more jurisdictions adopt the same approach, the greater the reduction in complexity, uncertainty and risks of double taxation and unintended non-taxation.

B.4. Commentary on applying the general rule – Supply of a service or intangible to a legal entity with single location ("single location entity" – "SLE")

3.41   For the purposes of this section, the businesses to which the general rule applies are assumed to be separate legal entities, whether related by common ownership or not. These legal entities are located solely in their respective jurisdictions and have no business presence elsewhere.

3.42   Under the general rule for business-to-business supplies, the place of the customer's location serves as a proxy for the jurisdiction of business use. The result of applying this general rule is that the jurisdiction where the customer is located has the taxing rights over services and intangibles supplied across international borders.

3.43   In order to support a satisfactory application of the general rule to single location entities, this section considers its application from the perspectives of the supplier, customer and tax administrations. Examples 1 and 2 in the Annex I to this Chapter provide relatively straightforward illustrations of how this general rule operates. Examples 3, 4 and 5 in the Annex I illustrate how this general rule is applied in more complex situations.

B.4.1. Supplies to single location entities – Supplier

3.44   In a business-to-business environment, it is reasonable to assume that suppliers will normally have developed a relationship with their customers. This will be particularly so in cases where supplies of services or intangibles are made on an on-going basis or in cases where one supply is made and the value of that supply is significant enough to warrant the development of business agreements such as contracts.

3.45   The principal effect of the general rule on suppliers is that they need to identify and be able to demonstrate who their customer is in order to make the supply free of VAT in their jurisdiction if the customer is located outside the supplier's jurisdiction. Once satisfied that the customer is a business and is located in another jurisdiction, the supplier makes that supply free of VAT in its jurisdiction as, under the general rule, the taxing rights over that supply are in the jurisdiction of the customer's location.

3.46   In many cases this will be straightforward and can be determined by reference to the business agreement. The nature of the service or intangible being supplied and the wording used in any supporting documentation may also contribute to verification of the international and business nature of the supply.

3.47   To avoid unnecessary burdens on suppliers, it is recommended that the customer be liable to account for any tax due. This can be achieved through the reverse charge mechanism (sometimes referred to as "tax shift" or "self-assessment") where that is consistent with the overall design of the national consumption tax system.[26] Accordingly, the supplier should then not be required to be identified for VAT or account for tax in the customer's jurisdiction.

3.48   The general rule applies in any situation where the supplier and customer are separate legal entities irrespective of whether they are related through any form of common ownership, management or control.

3.49   The application of the general rule will not be affected by the circumstance that the supplier i) supplies a customer who supplies onwards the services or intangibles to a third party,[27] or ii) directly provides the services or intangibles to a third party that is not the customer under the business agreement or iii) is paid by a third party that is not the customer under the business agreement. This is explained in further detail in the following paragraphs.

B.4.1.1. The determination of the place of taxation is not affected by any onward supply

3.50   It is common for multinational businesses to centralise certain procurement activities in one jurisdiction in order to obtain the economic benefits of single large agreements as opposed to multiple lower value agreements. These are generally referred to as "global" agreements. The central procurement company then supplies onwards the supplies or parts of the supplies to the various related businesses around the world.

3.51   The onward supply of those services to related businesses will be covered by separate business agreements entered into between the central procurement company and each of the related businesses. If the related businesses are the customers under those business agreements, the taxing rights over these onward supplies will be in the jurisdictions where these

---

26. For the purposes of these Guidelines, the "reverse charge mechanism" is a tax mechanism that switches the liability to pay the tax from the supplier to the customer. If the customer is entitled to full input tax credit in respect of this supply, it may be that local VAT legislation does not require the reverse charge to be made. Tax administrations are encouraged to publicise their approach.

27. For the purposes of these Guidelines, a third party is an entity recognised as a "business". "Third party" refers to a party other than the supplier or the customer and has no necessary correlation to its meaning in other contexts, including direct taxation.

related businesses are located, in accordance with the general rule. If these jurisdictions operate a reverse charge mechanism, these related businesses will be liable to account for any VAT at the rate applicable in their jurisdictions.

3.52   The procurement company may well supply a business located in the same jurisdiction as the original supplier (see Annex I to this Chapter – Example 3). When one applies the general rule, the place of taxation should be decided for each supply individually so that the determination of the place of taxation of services or intangibles for VAT purposes will not be affected by any subsequent supply or lack of such supply. The supplier should accordingly determine the identity of the customer by reference to the relevant business agreement. Where the customer is located in another jurisdiction, the supplier is entitled to make the supply free of VAT. As long as there is no evasion or avoidance, the fact that the customer subsequently supplies the services or intangibles onwards to a third party business is not, in itself, relevant, even where the third party business is located in the jurisdiction of the supplier.

B.4.1.2. The determination of the place of taxation is not affected by the direct provision of the services or intangibles to a third party business other than the customer of the supply

3.53   The supplier may also be required under the terms of the business agreement to provide services or intangibles directly to a third party (see Annex I to this Chapter – Example 3). As long as there is no evasion or avoidance, the customer remains the customer identified in the business agreement and it is this customer's location that determines the place of taxation. The mere direct provision of the supply to a third party business does not, in itself, affect that outcome. Accordingly, the general rule should be applied in such a way that the supplier makes a supply free of VAT to a foreign customer even if the third party business is located in the same jurisdiction as the supplier.

B.4.1.3. The determination of the place of taxation is not affected by the direction of the payment flows and the identity and location of the payer

3.54   Particular care may be required where payment flows differ from the flows of services or intangibles. Typically, a customer pays a supplier for services or intangibles supplied under a business agreement. However, there may be circumstances where another party may pay for that supply. For instance, it is common for multinational groups of businesses to reduce costs by appointing a company within a group to be the "paymaster"[28] responsible

---

28. This company may be referred to as a "paymaster", "cash clearing agent", "billing agent" or some other such term. These Guidelines use the term "paymaster".

for payments under the relevant agreement to pay for services and intangibles acquired. In such cases, services or intangibles supplied by the supplier or the supplier's foreign subsidiaries to foreign customers may be paid for by the customer's parent business located in the supplier's jurisdiction, although the supplies may not be made to the parent business (See Annex I to this Chapter – Example 5). When the general rule is applied, the place of taxation should be decided for each supply individually. The direction of the payment flows and the identity and location of the payer are not, in themselves, relevant. The payment flows are consideration for the supplies under the relevant business agreements but do not, in themselves, create additional supplies, alter the supplies, nor identify the customer or customer location. Accordingly, the supplier makes the supply to the customer identified in the relevant business agreement and the place of taxation is that customer's location. As long as there is no evasion or avoidance, the supplier is therefore entitled to make a supply free of VAT to a foreign customer even if that supply is paid by a third party business located in the same jurisdiction as the supplier.

B.4.2. Supplies to single location entities – Customer

3.55   It is recommended that the customer be liable to account for any tax due under the reverse charge mechanism where that is consistent with the overall design of the national consumption tax system. Under this procedure, the customer is typically required to declare the VAT due on the supply received from the foreign supplier as output tax on the relevant VAT return. The rate to be applied is the rate applicable in the customer's jurisdiction. The customer is then entitled to input tax deduction to the extent allowed under the rules of its jurisdiction.

3.56   If the customer is entitled to full input tax deduction on the relevant supply, it may be that local VAT legislation does not require declaration of the output tax under the reverse charge mechanism. This is an option provided in some jurisdictions and businesses in this position should ensure that they are aware of their jurisdiction's requirements in this respect. Similarly, some jurisdictions may employ a type of VAT that does not require application of a reverse charge as it would not suit the nature of the tax as applied. Businesses importing services and intangibles from a foreign supplier should ensure that they are familiar with their domestic legislation and administrative practices.

3.57   The customer is obliged to pay any tax due on the supply under the reverse charge mechanism where that is consistent with the overall design of the national consumption tax system. The customer is liable to pay even where i) the customer supplies onwards the services or intangibles to a third party ii) the services or intangibles are not directly provided to the customer or iii) the customer does not pay for the supply. This is explained in further detail in the following paragraphs.

B.4.2.1. The determination of the place of taxation is not affected by any onward supply

3.58   As stated in paragraph 3.50, it may be that the customer supplies onwards the services or intangibles from the foreign supplier as separate supplies (e.g. within a "global" agreement). As long as there is no evasion or avoidance, the place of taxation for these supplies should be decided for each supply individually and the original international supply is not affected (see Annex I to this Chapter – Example 3). The general rule continues to apply. It is likely that the customer when supplying onwards the supplies or parts of the supplies to related businesses will have entered into business agreements with those businesses. If the related businesses are the customers under those business agreements, the taxing rights over these onward supplies will be in the jurisdictions where these related businesses are located, in accordance with the general rule. If these jurisdictions operate a reverse charge mechanism, these related businesses will be liable to account for any VAT at the rate applicable in their jurisdictions.

B.4.2.2. The determination of the place of taxation is not affected by the direct provision of the services or intangibles to a third party business other than the customer of the supply

3.59   As described in paragraph 3.53, the customer may, under the terms of the relevant business agreement, require that the services or intangibles be provided directly to a third party. Even if that third party is located in a different jurisdiction from that of the customer identified in the business agreement, the place of taxation remains in the jurisdiction where the customer identified in the business agreement is located. If this jurisdiction operates a reverse charge mechanism, this customer identified in the business agreement will be liable to account for any VAT at the rate applicable in its jurisdiction (see Annex I to this Chapter – Example 3).

B.4.2.3. The determination of the place of taxation is not affected by the direction of the payment flows and the identity and location of the payer

3.60   As described in paragraph 3.54, multinational business groups may appoint a group member to act as paymaster for services or intangibles supplied to the group (i.e. a "paymaster" agreement). Consequently, the customer is not the party who pays the supplier for the supply under the business agreement. In such situations the direction of the payment flows and the identity and location of the payer are not, in themselves, relevant. The supply is to the customer identified in the relevant business agreement and the place of taxation is that customer's location (see Annex I to this Chapter – Example 5).

B.4.3. Supplies to single location entities – Tax administrations

3.61   The growth in international supplies of services and intangibles has led to increased complexity for tax administrations as well as for businesses. The intangible nature of many services is such that the comparative simplicity for goods (exports relieved, imports taxed) cannot be replicated with respect to services and intangibles. It is, therefore, important that tax administrations make it clear to both businesses and to staff responsible for carrying out compliance checks and audits what the rules are in their own jurisdiction and that they should be applied according to the facts of each individual supply.

3.62   Under the general rule supplies of services and intangibles are subject to tax according to the rules of the jurisdiction where the customer is located. This means that a supplier of international business-to-business services and intangibles makes such supplies free of VAT in its jurisdiction. The tax administration of the supplier may require the supplier to produce evidence that the customer is a business and that this business is located in another jurisdiction. To minimise compliance burdens on the supplier, tax administrations are encouraged to provide businesses with clear guidance on the evidence they require.

3.63   It is recommended that the customer be liable to account for any VAT due to its local tax administration under the reverse charge mechanism where that is consistent with the overall design of the national consumption tax system. Tax administrations are encouraged to make businesses aware of the need to account for any tax on "imported" services and intangibles from their suppliers in other jurisdictions. The normal domestic rate applicable to the nature of the services or intangibles involved should be applied. If the customer is entitled to full input tax credit in respect of this supply, it may be that local VAT legislation does not require the reverse charge to be declared on the local VAT return. In such cases tax administrations are encouraged to publicise this to business. Jurisdictions that require this declaration are likewise encouraged to make it clear that tax is required to be accounted for in this way.[29]

3.64   The reverse charge mechanism has a number of advantages. First, the tax authority in the jurisdiction of business use can verify and ensure compliance since that authority has personal jurisdiction over the customer. Second, the compliance burden is largely shifted from the supplier to the customer and is minimised since the customer has full access to the details of the supply. Third,

---

29. In cases where a customer omits to account properly for such a reverse charge, but is still, nevertheless, entitled to full input tax deduction in respect of that supply, it is recommended that any penalties that might be applied should be proportionate and linked to the gravity of the failure made, where the gravity of the failure is a consideration, bearing in mind there is no net revenue loss.

the administrative costs for the tax authority are also lower because the supplier is not required to comply with tax obligations in the customer's jurisdiction (e.g. VAT identification, audits, which would otherwise have to be administered, and translation and language barriers). Finally, it reduces the revenue risks associated with the collection of tax by non-resident suppliers, whether or not that supplier's customers are entitled to deduct the input tax.

3.65   The determination of the place of taxation of services or intangibles for VAT purposes should be decided for each supply individually. As long as there is no evasion or avoidance, it will, therefore, not be affected by i) any subsequent onward supply or lack of such supply, ii) the direct provision of the services or intangibles to a third party business other than the customer or iii) by the direction of the payment flows and the identity and location of the payer. This is explained in further detail in the following paragraphs.

B.4.3.1. The determination of the place of taxation is not affected by any onward supply

3.66   As stated in paragraphs 3.50 and 3.58, businesses with related separate legal entities in other jurisdictions may supply onwards the services or intangibles they have bought in within a "global" agreement from foreign to other related companies. These supplies should be subject to the normal VAT rules, including the general rule in respect of international services and intangibles (see Annex I to this Chapter – Example 3). Accordingly, it is recommended that:

● the tax administration in the supplier's jurisdiction allow the supplier to make a supply free of VAT, providing the supplier can identify the customer and demonstrate that the customer is located abroad;

● the tax administration in the customer's jurisdiction ensures that the customer accounts for any tax due on the supply from the foreign supplier, using the reverse charge mechanism where that is consistent with the overall design of the national consumption tax system.

B.4.3.2. The determination of the place of taxation is not affected by the direct provision of the services or intangibles to a third party business other than the customer of the supply

3.67   As stated in paragraphs 3.53 and 3.59, even if some or all of the services or intangibles are not directly provided in the jurisdiction of the customer but rather are directly provided in another jurisdiction such as, for instance, the jurisdiction of the supplier or of a third party business, the general rule continues to apply (see Annex I to this Chapter – Example 3). The customer's jurisdiction remains the jurisdiction with the taxing rights. For example, an accountancy firm may have entered into a business agreement with a customer located in another jurisdiction but may perform much of the work in its own jurisdiction and also provide its services directly to a third party business. As long as there is no evasion or avoidance, this does not, in itself, prevent the place of taxation from being the customer's location. Accordingly it is recommended that:

- the tax administration in the supplier's jurisdiction does not seek tax from the supplier based entirely on the fact that the supplier is directly providing the services or intangibles there, but allows it to make a supply free of VAT to the foreign customer identified in the business agreement;

- the tax administration in the customer's jurisdiction ensures that the customer accounts for any tax due on the supply from the foreign supplier, using the reverse charge mechanism, even if the services or intangibles were directly provided by a local third party business.

B.4.3.3. The determination of the place of taxation is not affected by the direction of the payment flows and the identity and location of the payer

3.68   Paragraphs 3.54 and 3.60 recognise that there may be situations where another party pays for the supply to the customer in the business agreement (see Annex Ito this Chapter – Example 5). That third party business is usually referred to in multinational groups as the group "paymaster" and may not be supplied with any services or intangibles itself. Regardless of where that third party business is located, the services or intangibles are supplied to the customer identified in the relevant business agreement and the taxing rights belong to the jurisdiction in which that customer is located. Accordingly it is recommended that:

- the tax administration in the supplier's jurisdiction does not seek tax from the supplier based entirely on the fact that the paymaster third party business is located there, but allows it to make the supply free of VAT to the foreign customer identified in the business agreement;

- the tax administration in the customer's jurisdiction ensures that the customer accounts for any tax due on the supply from the foreign supplier, using the reverse charge mechanism, even if the supply is paid for by a third party business.

3.69   The foregoing approach leads to a logical result because supplies are subject to tax in the jurisdiction in which the services or intangibles are used by the business in accordance with the destination principle as implemented by the general rule and there is neither double taxation nor unintended non-taxation in any of the jurisdictions involved.

3.70   Annex I to this Chapter provides examples of how the general rule on place of taxation for business-to-business supplies of services and intangibles to single location entities, can be applied in practice.

B.5. Commentary on applying the recharge method under the general rule – Supply of a service or intangible to a legal entity with multiple locations ("multiple location entity" – "MLE")

3.71   Guideline 3.4 recommends that taxing rights over a supply of a service or intangible to a MLE accrue to the jurisdiction(s) where the establishment(s) using the service or intangible is (are) located. It is recognised that a number of possible approaches could be used to identify which establishment of the customer MLE is regarded as using a service or intangible and where this establishment is located. The following broad categories of approaches can be distinguished:

- direct use approach, which focuses directly on the establishment that uses the service or intangible.
- direct delivery approach, which focuses on the establishment to which the service or intangible is delivered.
- recharge method, which focuses on the establishment that uses the service or intangible as determined on the basis of internal recharge arrangements within the MLE, made in accordance with corporate tax, accounting or other regulatory requirements.

3.72   Paragraphs 3.25 to 3.40 provide a broad description of these approaches and their possible use in practice. This Commentary looks in further detail at the recharge method, as tax administrations may be less familiar with the possible operation of this method than with other approaches.

3.73   The recharge method requires MLEs to internally recharge the costs of externally acquired services or intangibles to their establishments that use these services or intangibles, as supported by internal recharge arrangements. Under the recharge method, these internal recharges are used as a basis for allocating the taxing rights over such services or intangibles to the jurisdiction(s) where the establishment(s) using this service or intangible is (are) located.

3.74   This can be achieved by following a two-step approach:

- The first step follows the business agreement between the external supplier and the MLE. The taxing rights over the supply to the MLE are allocated to the jurisdiction of the customer establishment that represents the MLE in the business agreement with the supplier.
- The second step is required when the service or intangible is used wholly or partially by one or more other establishments than the establishment that has represented the MLE in the business agreement with the supplier. This second step follows the internal recharge made by the MLE for allocating the external cost of the service or intangible to the establishment, or establishments, using this service or intangible. This internal recharge is

used as the basis for allocating the taxing rights over the service or intangible to the jurisdiction where these establishment(s) of use is (are) located, by treating this internal recharge of the externally acquired service or intangible as within the scope of VAT.

3.75   The following sections consider the application of the recharge method from the perspectives of the supplier, customer and tax administrations. Annex II to this Chapter provides an example of how the recharge method could be applied in practice.

B.5.1. First step – Supply to the MLE

B.5.1.1. Supplier

3.76   As is the case for any supply, the supplier will need to identify and be able to demonstrate who the customer is and where this customer is located in order to determine where the taxing rights will accrue.

3.77   Under the first step of the recharge method, the taxing rights are allocated to the jurisdiction of the establishment that represents the MLE in the business agreement with the supplier. The various elements of the business agreement with the supplier should identify this establishment and where it is located. Once satisfied that this establishment is located in a jurisdiction other than the supplier's, the supplier will be entitled to make the supply free of VAT in its jurisdiction.

B.5.1.2. Customer

3.78   Where the customer's establishment that has represented the MLE in the business agreement is located in a jurisdiction other than the supplier's, it is recommended that this establishment be liable for any tax due on the transaction. This can be achieved through the reverse charge mechanism (also referred to as "tax shift" or "self-assessment") where this is consistent with the overall design of the national consumption tax system. Under this procedure, this customer's establishment will typically be required to declare the tax due on the supply received from the foreign supplier as output tax on the relevant VAT return. The rate to be applied will be the normal domestic rate applicable to the nature of the service or intangible in the jurisdiction of the customer's establishment. The customer's establishment that makes the recharge will deduct the related input tax in line with the normal rules that ensure VAT neutrality.

3.79   If the customer establishment that has represented the MLE in the business agreement is entitled to full input tax credit in respect of this supply, it may be that local VAT legislation does not require the reverse charge to be made.

B.5.1.3. Tax administrations

3.80   The tax administration in the jurisdiction of the supplier will need to know the nature of the supply as well as the identity of the customer and the jurisdiction in which the customer is located. Where the service or intangible is supplied to a business located in another jurisdiction, this supply will be made free of VAT in the jurisdiction of the supplier. The supplier will therefore need to hold all the relevant information that constitutes the business agreement to demonstrate the nature of the supply and the identity of the customer. Where this customer is a MLE, under the recharge method the business agreement will need to provide evidence of the identity of the establishment that represents the MLE in the business agreement and the location of this establishment. Tax administrations are encouraged to provide businesses with clear guidance on the evidence they require.

3.81   The customer's establishment that has represented the MLE in the business agreement with the supplier will account for any VAT due to its local tax administration under the reverse charge mechanism where that is consistent with the overall design of the national consumption tax system. Tax administrations are encouraged to make businesses aware of the need to account for any tax on "imported" services or intangibles from suppliers in other jurisdictions, including if these services or intangibles are acquired by an establishment of a MLE.

3.82   If the customer's establishment is entitled to full input tax credit in respect of this supply, it may be that local VAT legislation would not require the reverse charge to be made. In such cases tax administrations are also encouraged to publicise this.

B.5.2. Second step – Recharge to the establishment(s) of use

B.5.2.1. Supplier

3.83   The external supplier of the service or intangible to the MLE has no involvement in the recharge of the service or intangible to the customer's establishment of use. This is the sole responsibility of the customer MLE.

B.5.2.2. Customer

3.84   The customer's establishment that has entered into the business agreement with the external supplier will either have acquired the service or intangible for its own use or will have acquired it wholly or partially for use by other establishments of the customer MLE. In the latter case, the customer establishment that has represented the MLE in the business agreement with the external supplier is required to subsequently charge the other establishment(s) of the MLE using the service or intangible. Under the recharge method, this internal charge of the external service or intangible is treated as consideration for a supply within the scope of VAT.

3.85   There will be no recharge if the service or intangible was acquired by an establishment of the MLE for its own use.

3.86   Whether or not there will be a recharge for a service or intangible acquired by an establishment of a MLE for use wholly or partially by another establishment of this MLE in the same jurisdiction, will depend on the internal rules of this jurisdiction. This Commentary deals only with cross-border supplies of services and intangibles.

3.87   As for any other supply, the establishment of recharge will need to identify and be able to demonstrate which is the establishment of use and where this establishment is located.

3.88   Under the recharge method, MLEs will need to have internal arrangements in place to support and facilitate the internal charges between their different establishments. MLEs and tax administrations will rely on these internal arrangements to provide them with the information that would otherwise be covered by a business agreement. These internal arrangements are hereafter referred to as recharge arrangements for the purpose of the application of the recharge method.

3.89   The various elements of the recharge arrangement should facilitate the identification of the establishment of recharge and the establishment(s) of use to which an internal recharge is made and should provide sufficient information to evidence a consistent and correct VAT treatment of the recharge.

3.90   This may be straightforward in many cases, particularly where MLEs have adopted an arrangement where specific services or intangibles acquired externally are recharged as such to the establishment of use. This may for instance be the case for large expenses that can be isolated and charged to the establishment of use, for example in installing a new computer system or performing a major upgrade. Such arrangements are of great practical convenience, as they allow the service or intangible that is recharged as well as the basis for the recharge to be clearly identified. MLEs are encouraged to adopt such arrangements as much as possible for their internal recharges.

3.91   It is recognised however that it will not always be possible to adopt this approach in practice. This may be the case, for instance, where a service or intangible is acquired for use by multiple establishments and a separate recording of use by each of the establishments would be disproportionately burdensome. This may occur where legal services or marketing services are acquired centrally for several establishments of a MLE. A detailed analysis of these services and their use by each of the establishments may be difficult or overly burdensome in certain circumstances. In such cases, MLEs may find it necessary to use cost allocation or apportionment methods that include a certain degree of estimation or approximation of the actual use of the service by each establishment.

3.92   Tax administrations that implement the recharge method are encouraged to allow such cost allocation or apportionment methods where the straightforward recharge for specific services or intangibles would be disproportionately burdensome and to provide businesses with clear guidance on the allocation or apportionment approaches that they consider allowable.

3.93   Such cost allocation or apportionment methods (allocation keys) should be "fair and reasonable", in that they should produce recharges that are commensurate with the reasonably expected use by the establishments of use, follow sound accounting principles and contain safeguards against manipulation. Where possible, information that is already available for accounting and tax and other regulatory purposes should be used. There is no single solution that would be appropriate in all cases. What is "fair and reasonable" depends not only on the type of service but also on the size and structure of a company, the sector and the complexity of the business environment in which it operates. Whatever allocation key is used, it should be capable of being justified and applied consistently without creating undue compliance and administrative burden for businesses and tax administrations.

3.94   Commonly used allocation keys include: number of employees, square meters of office space, number of fleet cars, computer usage, advertising expenses, number of accounting entries, number of invoices processed, etc. A clear, directly measurable allocation key may not always be available, for example in relation to legal expenses, general systems maintenance, etc. In such cases, it is not uncommon for costs to be allocated on the basis of the respective size of the establishments.

3.95   It is important for the proper operation of the recharge method that the relationship between the initial supply of the service or intangible to the MLE (first step) and the onward recharge to the establishment(s) of use (second step) does not become obscured. The objective of the recharge method is to ensure that taxing rights over supplies to an MLE are effectively allocated to the jurisdiction where the establishment of use is located. The MLE will therefore be expected to ensure that tax administrations can reasonably establish the relationship between the initial supply and the recharge and that they can notably establish the link between the price of the initial supply and the amount of the recharge, without requiring a recharge on a transaction-by-transaction basis.

3.96   The establishment of recharge will be entitled to make the recharge free of VAT in its jurisdiction on the basis of the information available in the recharge arrangement, as the other establishment(s) will be located in other jurisdictions. The elements of the recharge arrangement should demonstrate which establishment(s) is (are) using the service and its (their) location in another jurisdiction. It is recommended that the establishment of recharge issue a document equivalent to an invoice for the recharge to the establishment(s) of use.

3.97   To ensure VAT neutrality for the establishment that makes the recharge, general input VAT deduction rules should apply for this establishment in respect of the input VAT on the service or intangible received and subsequently recharged. The application of the recharge method should not influence the MLE's right to input VAT deduction in respect of purchases other than the service or intangible to which the recharge method is applied.

3.98   It is recommended that the establishment of use be liable for any tax due on the recharge. This can be achieved through reverse charge mechanisms (also referred to as "tax shift" or "self-assessment") where this is consistent with the overall design of the national consumption tax system. It may be that local VAT legislation does not require the reverse charge to be made.

3.99   When a service or intangible is used wholly by an establishment other than the one that represented the MLE in the business agreement, the taxable amount would in principle be the amount of the recharge that corresponds to the purchase price of the service or intangible.

3.100   Where the service or intangible is used by several establishments, the taxable amount for each establishment would in principle be the part of the purchase price of the service or intangible that is recharged to this establishment on the basis of an acceptable apportionment or allocation approach.

3.101   The taxable amount should be evidenced by the recharge arrangement. The rate to be applied would in principle be the normal domestic rate applicable to the nature of the service or intangible in the jurisdiction of the customer's establishment of use. This customer's establishment would then be entitled to deduct input tax to the extent allowed under the rules of its jurisdiction.

3.102   Where the recharge of a service or intangible purchased from an external supplier is bundled with an internal cost charge (e.g. salary expense of internally supplied services), it is for the MLE to separate the cost of the externally purchased service or intangible from the other costs and to evidence the internal character of these other costs if this would be necessary to ensure that the recharge method is applied only on the cost of the externally purchased service or intangible.

B.5.2.3. Tax administrations

3.103   Tax administrations are encouraged to provide clear guidance to businesses on the operation of the recharge method, including its scope, the allocation or apportionment approaches that they consider acceptable and the documentation requirements to support this method, the input VAT deduction rules to ensure VAT neutrality for the establishment that makes the recharge, the time of taxation rules to be applied to the internal recharge and the process to account for any tax due on an internal recharge.

3.104   In line with normal audit policies, tax administrations will need an audit trail that enables them, when necessary, to review commercial documentation down to the transaction level in order to identify the nature of the individual service that is recharged and thus to determine whether the place of taxation, the taxable amount and the applicable rate of tax are correct.

3.105   This documentation may include a copy of the original invoice from the external supplier, the allocation method and allocation key used and any other documents or electronic records that show how the VAT was calculated (e.g. distinction between recharge of external costs and internal added value), the documentation from the establishment that makes the recharge requesting payment (i.e. document equivalent to an invoice), accounting entries and documentation supporting the payment by the establishment of use.

3.106   In cases where the separation of external costs from other costs within an internal recharge would be necessary to ensure that the recharge method is applied only on the cost of the externally purchased service or intangible, tax administrations may wish to allow methods that include a certain degree of approximation, notably if a detailed separation would be considered disproportionally burdensome (e.g. in view of the limited amounts involved).

3.107   In addition, it will in principle also be necessary for auditors at the tax administration in the jurisdiction of use to satisfy themselves that:

● Any cross-border recharge of external costs between establishments has been treated as within the scope of VAT.

● Establishments have accounted for VAT correctly on any such recharge, including where netting has taken place.[30]

● The establishment of use has accounted for VAT as if a recharge arrangement were in place, in cases where a service has been purchased by another establishment in a different jurisdiction and the establishment of use has not been recharged even though this recharge was required.

---

30. Netting occurs when establishments that have mutual obligations, e.g. because they have each made recharges to each other, agree to compensate the value of both obligations and to pay only the net amount that is still owed by one of the establishments after this compensation. Where netting has taken place, VAT should in principle be applied on the taxable amount of each recharge and not just the net value.

3.108   Where possible, tax administrations should use information that is already available for accounting or tax and other regulatory purposes, to avoid creation of new methodologies and processes purely for VAT purposes.

3.109   It is recommended that any tax due on the internal recharge of a service or intangible purchased from an external supplier be accounted for by the MLE's establishment of use. This can be achieved through reverse charge mechanisms where this is consistent with the overall design of the national consumption tax system. However, it is recognised that local VAT legislation may not require the reverse charge to be made if the establishment of use is entitled to full input tax credit in respect of this supply. In such cases, the tax administration is encouraged to publicise this. Jurisdictions that do require a reverse charge to be made are likewise recommended to make this clear.

C. Business-to-consumer supplies – The general rules

C.1. Introduction

3.110   It is theoretically more straightforward in the business-to-consumer[31] context than in the business-to-business context to implement the destination principle, as set out in Guideline 3.1, to ensure that tax on services and intangibles is ultimately levied only in the jurisdiction where the final consumption occurs. In the business-to-business context, the place of taxation rules should facilitate the ultimate goal of taxing business-to-consumer supplies in the jurisdiction where final consumption occurs, while at the same time ensuring that the burden of the tax does not rest on either business, unless intentionally provided by legislation (see Guideline 2.1). In the business-to-consumer context, the objective is simply to tax the final consumption in the jurisdiction where it occurs with the tax burden resting on the final consumer. Accordingly, the primary objective for place of taxation rules in the business-to-consumer context is to predict with reasonable accuracy the place where the services or intangibles are likely to be consumed while taking into account practical constraints, and ideally such place of taxation rules should be simple and practical for taxpayers to apply, for customers to understand and for tax administrations to administer.

3.111   Achieving this objective for business-to-consumer supplies of services was reasonably easy in the past, when consumers typically purchased services from local suppliers and those supplies generally involved services that could be expected to be consumed in the jurisdiction where they were

---

31. For the purposes of the Guidelines, business-to-consumer supplies are assumed to be supplies where the customer is not recognised as a business. Such recognition may include the treatment for VAT purposes specifically or in national law more generally (notably in jurisdictions that have not implemented a VAT). See also paragraphs 3.7 and 3.8.

performed.[32] Consequently, some jurisdictions chose to implement VAT systems that determined the place of taxation for such services primarily by reference to the supplier's location, on the assumption that this was where these services were normally performed and where final consumers were actually located when consuming the service. A place of taxation rule based on the supplier's location was often supplemented by a place of taxation rule based on place of performance or other proxies, for cases in which the supplier's location was a less reliable indicator of the location where services were likely to be consumed (e.g. entertainment or sporting events). Over time, a range of services developed for which the supplier's location or the place of performance was used less often to determine the place of taxation and as a consequence the applicability of other rules increased, notably referring to the customer's location. At the same time, VAT systems were implemented in certain jurisdictions that determined the place of taxation using an iterative application of multiple proxies, and such jurisdictions often favoured the customer's location as the key proxy for determining the place of taxation for both business-to-business and business-to-consumer supplies. Still other jurisdictions used a very broad place of effective consumption rule to determine the place of taxation. As a result of these different approaches, there was a lack of consistency and clarity about which jurisdiction should have the right to tax particular supplies of services and intangibles.

3.112   The emergence of the global economy, with its growing reliance on digital supplies, created further challenges for these traditional approaches to determining the place of taxation for business-to-consumer supplies of services and intangibles. Advances in technology and trade liberalisation increasingly enabled businesses to supply services and intangibles to customers around the world, leading to a strong growth in international business-to-consumer trade in remotely supplied services and intangibles. These developments created challenges for VAT systems that used a proxy based on the supplier's location or the place of performance to determine the place of taxation. Where services or intangibles can be supplied remotely to customers who may be located anywhere in the world when they consume the service or intangible, the supplier's location and the place of performance are less likely to accurately predict the likely place of consumption. Place of taxation rules based on those proxies are thus unlikely to lead to an appropriate result. Moreover, often the actual place of performance might be unclear. For example, a technician in one country might take control of a computer in another country to resolve an issue using key strokes performed thousands of kilometres from the computer, using

---

32. This paragraph refers only to supplies of services rather than to supplies of services and intangibles, because services constituted the overwhelming proportion of such supplies to final consumers in the past.

information and communication infrastructure located in a number of different jurisdictions. In such a case, it could be difficult to reach a consistent conclusion on whether the place of performance is where the technician is, where the computer is or somewhere in between.

3.113   For supplies of services and intangibles whose consumption bears no necessary relationship to the location in which the supply is performed and in which the person performing the supply is located, a rule based on the customer's usual residence is the most appropriate approach for determining the place of taxation in a business-to-consumer context. The place in which customers have their usual residence is used by VAT systems around the world as a proxy for predicting the place of consumption of many types of services and intangibles supplied to final consumers. This approach reflects the presumption that final consumers ordinarily consume services and intangibles in the jurisdiction where they have their usual residence and it provides a clear connection to a readily identifiable place. It ensures that the services and intangibles acquired by final consumers from foreign suppliers are taxed on the same basis and at the same rate as domestic supplies, in accordance with Guideline 2.4 on VAT neutrality in international trade (see Chapter 2). There is therefore no tax advantage for final consumers in buying from low or no tax jurisdictions. A place of taxation rule based on the customer's usual residence is also reasonably practical for suppliers to apply, provided that a simplified registration and compliance regime is available (see Sections C.3.2 and C.3.3). It is also reasonably practical for tax administrations to administer, provided that it is supported by effective international co-operation in tax administration and enforcement (see Section C.3.4).

3.114   Against this background, two general rules are recommended for determining the place of taxation for business-to-consumer supplies of services and intangibles:

● for supplies that are physically performed at a readily identifiable place and that are ordinarily consumed at the same time and place where they are physically performed in the presence of both the person performing the supply and the person consuming it ("on-the-spot supplies"), Guideline 3.5 recommends a place of taxation rule based on the place of performance;

● for supplies that are not covered by Guideline 3.5, Guideline 3.6 recommends a place of taxation rule based on the customer's usual residence.[33]

---

33. Under the general rule for business-to-business supplies of services and intangibles set out in Guideline 3.2 and under the general rule for business-to-consumer supplies of services and intangibles set out in Guideline 3.6, the place of taxation is thus determined by reference to the customer's location. The customer's location is determined by reference to the customer's business establishment in the business-to-business context (in accordance with Guideline 3.2) and to the customer's usual residence in the business-to-consumer context (in accordance with Guideline 3.6).

3.115   These general rules effectively result in the allocation of the taxing rights over business-to-consumer supplies of services and intangibles to the jurisdiction where it can reasonably be assumed that the final consumer is actually located when consuming the supply. This is the place where the final consumer consumes the on-the-spot supply, or the final consumer's usual residence where he or she is presumed to consume a remotely supplied service or intangible.

C.2. Business-to-consumer supplies – On-the-spot supplies

3.116   The place of physical performance of the supply is the appropriate proxy to determine the place of consumption for on-the-spot supplies of services and intangibles to final consumers. For the purposes of these Guidelines, on-the-spot supplies are services and intangibles that are normally physically performed at a readily identifiable place and are ordinarily consumed at the same time and place where they are physically performed, and that ordinarily require the presence of both the person performing the supply and the person consuming it. As well as providing a reasonably accurate indication of the place of consumption, a place of taxation rule based on the place of physical performance is simple and practical for suppliers to apply and for tax administrations to administer.

> **Guideline 3.5**
>
> **For the application of Guideline 3.1, the jurisdiction in which the supply is physically performed has the taxing rights over business-to-consumer supplies of services and intangibles that**
>
> - **are physically performed at a readily identifiable place, and**
> - **are ordinarily consumed at the same time as and at the same place where they are physically performed, and**
> - **ordinarily require the physical presence of the person performing the supply and the person consuming the service or intangible at the same time and place where the supply of such a service or intangible is physically performed.**

3.117   Guideline 3.5 is aimed primarily at supplies that are typically consumed at an identifiable place where they are performed, rather than supplies that can be provided remotely or that can be consumed at a time and place other than the place of performance. Examples include services physically performed on the person (e.g. hairdressing, massage, beauty therapy, physiotherapy); accommodation; restaurant and catering services; entry to cinema, theatre performances, trade fairs, museums, exhibitions, and parks; attendance at sports competitions.[34]

3.118   The final consumption of these supplies ordinarily requires the physical presence of both the person performing the supply, who is usually the supplier, and the person consuming it. The application of Guideline 3.5 thus results in the allocation of the taxing rights to the jurisdiction where the final consumer is located when consuming the supply and where the person performing the supply is located at the time of final consumption.

3.119   On-the-spot supplies can be acquired by businesses as well as by private consumers. Jurisdictions could therefore adopt the approach that is recommended by Guideline 3.5 for business-to-consumer supplies, as a specific rule in the business-to-business context (see paragraphs 3.165-3.166). Such an approach would relieve suppliers of on-the-spot supplies, which are often small or medium businesses, of the compliance burden of having to distinguish between final consumers and businesses when making their taxing decision.[35]

C.3. Business-to-consumer supplies – Supplies of services and intangibles other than those covered by Guideline 3.5

3.120   For supplies of services and intangibles that lack an obvious connection with a readily identifiable place of physical performance and that are not ordinarily consumed at the place where they are physically performed in the presence of the person performing the supply and of the person consuming it, the place of physical performance generally does not provide a good indication of the likely place of consumption. This includes, for example, supplies of services and intangibles that are likely to be consumed at some time other than the time of performance, or for which the consumption and/or performance are likely to be ongoing, as well as services and intangibles that can easily be provided and consumed remotely.

3.121   For such business-to-consumer supplies of services and intangibles, the place of usual residence of the customer is a more appropriate

---

34. Jurisdictions that treat some of these items (such as accommodation and restaurant meals) as a supply of goods or some other category are encouraged to ensure consistency with these Guidelines by ensuring that such supplies are taxed at the place where they are performed. Similarly, where countries treat the supply of a ticket or right of entry as a separate supply, they are encouraged to determine the place of taxation by reference to place where the underlying supply of service is performed. See also footnote 17.

35. This should not be read as requiring countries to adopt such a categorisation approach to determining the place of taxation. Countries using an iterative approach may choose to use a series of rules that are applied consecutively to determine the appropriate place of taxation in an order the leads to the same end result as that recommended by Guideline 3.5.

proxy for the jurisdiction of consumption, as it can be assumed that these types of services and intangibles will ordinarily be consumed in the jurisdiction where the customer has his or her usual residence.

Guideline 3.6

For the application of Guideline 3.1, the jurisdiction in which the customer has its usual residence has the taxing rights over business-to-consumer supplies of services and intangibles other than those covered by Guideline 3.5.

3.122   Examples of supplies of services and intangibles that are not covered by Guideline 3.5 could include: consultancy, accountancy and legal services; financial and insurance services; telecommunication and broadcasting services; online supplies of software and software maintenance; online supplies of digital content (movies, TV shows, music, etc.); digital data storage; and online gaming.

C.3.1. Determining the jurisdiction of the usual residence of the customer

3.123   The jurisdiction in which the customer of a business-to-consumer supply has its usual residence is generally where the customer regularly lives or has established a home. Such customers are not considered to have their usual residence in a jurisdiction where they are only temporary, transitory visitors (e.g. as a tourist or as a participant to a training course or a conference).

3.124   Suppliers should be able to rely on information that is known or that can reasonably be known at the time when the tax treatment of the supply must be determined, thereby taking into account the different types of supplies and the circumstances in which such supplies are typically delivered.

3.125   The evidence available to suppliers about the jurisdiction in which the customer has its usual residence is likely to depend on the business model, the type and value of the supplies and on the suppliers' delivery model. Particularly in e-commerce, where activities often involve high volume, low-value supplies that rely on minimal interaction and communication between the supplier and its customer, it will often be difficult to determine the customer's place of usual residence from an agreement. Jurisdictions should provide clear and realistic guidance for suppliers on what is required to determine the place of usual residence of their customers in a business-to-consumer context.

3.126   In the business-to-consumer context, jurisdictions are encouraged to permit suppliers to rely, as much as possible, on information they routinely collect from their customers in the course of their normal business activity, as long as such information provides reasonably reliable evidence of the place of usual residence of their customers. In addition, jurisdictions could consider adopting rules that, if they are satisfied that a business is following these principles, this business should expect challenges only where there is misuse or abuse of such evidence. Any guidance provided by the tax authorities will need to take account of the law and practice in the relevant jurisdictions, including with regard to the protection of personal privacy, while maintaining flexibility for businesses.

3.127   Generally, the information provided by the customer may be considered as important evidence relevant to the determination of the jurisdiction of the customer's usual residence. This could include information collected within business processes (e.g. the ordering process), such as jurisdiction and address, bank details (notably country of the bank account), and credit card information. If needed jurisdictions may require that the reliability of such information be further supported through appropriate indicia of residence. In some cases, such indicia might be the only indication of the jurisdiction of the customer's usual residence. The available indicia will vary depending on the type of business or product involved, and might include the contact telephone number, the Internet Protocol address[36] of the device used to download digital content or the customer's trading history (which could, for example, include information on the predominant place of consumption, language of digital content supplied or billing address). These indicia are likely to evolve over time as technology and business practices develop.

C.3.2. VAT collection in cases where the supplier is not located in the jurisdiction of taxation

3.128   The correct charging, collection and remittance of VAT, and the associated reporting obligations are traditionally the responsibility of suppliers. While requiring suppliers to carry out these responsibilities is relatively straightforward in cases where the supplier is located in the jurisdiction of taxation, the matter could be more complex in cases where a business makes supplies that are taxable in a jurisdiction where it is not located. According to the traditional approach, the non-resident supplier is required to register in the jurisdiction of taxation and charge, collect and remit any tax due there. It is recognised, however, that it can often be complex and burdensome for non-resident suppliers to comply with such obligations in jurisdictions where they have no business presence, and equally difficult for tax administrations to enforce and administer them.

---

36. An Internet Protocol address, also known as an IP address, is a numerical label assigned to each device (e.g. computer, mobile phone) participating in a computer network that uses the Internet Protocol for communication.

3.129   For cross-border business-to-business supplies of services and intangibles that are taxable in the jurisdiction where the customer is located in accordance with Guideline 3.2, these Guidelines recommend the implementation of a reverse charge mechanism to minimise the administrative burden and complexity for non-resident suppliers, where this is consistent with the overall design of the national VAT system. If the customer is entitled to full input tax credit in respect of this supply, it may be that the local VAT legislation does not require the reverse charge to be made. The reverse charge mechanism shifts the liability to pay the tax from the supplier to the customer. Where only business-to-business supplies are involved, the application of the reverse charge mechanism should relieve the non-resident supplier of any requirement to be identified for VAT or to account for tax in the jurisdiction of taxation.

3.130   The reverse charge mechanism does not offer an appropriate solution for collecting VAT on business-to-consumer supplies of services and intangibles from non-resident suppliers. The level of compliance with a reverse charge mechanism for business-to-consumer supplies is likely to be low, since private consumers have little incentive to declare and pay the tax due, at least in the absence of meaningful sanctions for failing to comply with such an obligation. Moreover, enforcing the collection of small amounts of VAT from large numbers of private consumers is likely to involve considerable costs that would outweigh the revenue involved.

3.131   Work carried out by the OECD and other international organisations, as well as individual country experience, indicate that, at the present time, the most effective and efficient approach to ensure the appropriate collection of VAT on cross-border business-to-consumer supplies is to require the non-resident supplier to register and account for the VAT in the jurisdiction of taxation.

3.132   When implementing a registration-based collection mechanism for non-resident suppliers, it is recommended that jurisdictions consider establishing a simplified registration and compliance regime to facilitate compliance for non-resident suppliers. The highest feasible levels of compliance by non-resident suppliers are likely to be achieved if compliance obligations in the jurisdiction of taxation are limited to what is strictly necessary for the effective collection of the tax. Appropriate simplification is particularly important to facilitate compliance for businesses faced with obligations in multiple jurisdictions. Where traditional registration and compliance procedures are complex, their application for non-resident suppliers of business-to-consumer services and intangibles would risk creating barriers that may lead to non-compliance or to certain suppliers declining to serve customers in jurisdictions that impose such burdens.

3.133   A simplified registration and compliance regime for non-resident suppliers of business-to-consumer services and intangibles would operate separately from the traditional registration and compliance regime, without the same rights (e.g. input tax recovery) and obligations (e.g. full reporting) as a traditional regime. Experience with such simplified registration and compliance regimes has shown that they provide a practical and relatively effective solution for securing VAT revenues on business-to-consumer supplies of services and intangibles by non-resident suppliers, while minimising economic distortions and preserving neutrality between resident and non-resident suppliers. Such mechanisms allow tax administrations to capture a significant proportion of tax revenues associated with supplies to final consumers within their jurisdiction while incurring relatively limited administrative costs.

3.134   It is recognised that a proper balance needs to be struck between simplification and the needs of tax administrations to safeguard the revenue. Tax administrations need to ensure that the right amount of tax is collected and remitted from suppliers with which they might have no jurisdictional relationship. Against this background, Section C.3.3 below sets out the possible main features of a simplified registration and compliance regime for non-resident suppliers of business-to-consumer services and intangibles, balancing the need for simplification and the need of tax administrations to safeguard the revenue. This is intended to assist taxing jurisdictions[37] in evaluating and developing their framework for collecting VAT on business-to-consumer supplies of services and intangibles from non-resident suppliers with a view to increasing consistency among compliance processes across jurisdictions. Greater consistency among country approaches will further facilitate compliance, particularly by businesses that are faced with multi-jurisdictional obligations, reduce compliance costs and improve the effectiveness and quality of compliance processes. For tax authorities, consistency is also likely to support the effective international co-operation in tax administration and enforcement.

C.3.3. Main features of a simplified registration and compliance regime for non-resident suppliers

3.135   This section explores the key measures that taxing jurisdictions could take to simplify the administrative and compliance process of a registration-based collection regime for business-to-consumer supplies of services and intangibles by non-resident suppliers.

3.136   This section is intended to assist jurisdictions in evaluating and developing their framework for collecting VAT on business-to-consumer supplies of services and intangibles by non-resident businesses and to suggest the possible main features of a simplified registration and compliance regime.

---

37. For the purposes of these Guidelines, the taxing jurisdiction is the jurisdiction that is identified as the place of taxation in accordance with these Guidelines.

It also considers whether the scope of such a simplified registration and compliance regime could be extended to cross-border business-to-business supplies and recalls the proportionality principle as a guiding principle for the operation of a registration-based collection mechanism for non-resident suppliers. It identifies the possible simplification measures for each of the following core elements of a simplified administrative and compliance regime:

- Registration
- Input tax recovery – Refunds
- Returns
- Payments
- Record keeping
- Invoicing
- Availability of information
- Use of third-party service providers.

3.137   This section recognises the important role of technology for the simplification of administration and compliance. Many tax administrations have taken steps to exploit the use of technology to develop a range of electronic services to support their operations, in particular those concerned with tax collection processes and the provision of basic services to taxpayers. The reasons for this are fairly obvious: applied effectively, these technologies can deliver considerable benefits both to tax administrations and taxpayers (e.g. lower compliance and administrative costs and faster and more accessible services for taxpayers). But the use of technology will be effective only if the core elements of the administrative and compliance process are sufficiently clear and simple. This section therefore focuses mainly on possible simplification of administrative and compliance procedures while devoting less attention to technological features, recognising that these technologies are likely to continue to evolve over time.

C.3.3.1 Registration procedure

3.138   Simple registration procedures can be an important incentive for non-resident suppliers to engage with the tax authority of a jurisdiction where they might have no link other than the supply of services or intangibles to final consumers. The information requested could be limited to necessary details, which could include:

- Name of business, including the trading name
- Name of contact person responsible for dealing with tax administrations
- Postal and/or registered address of the business and its contact person

- Telephone number of contact person
- Electronic address of contact person
- Web sites URL of non-resident suppliers through which business is conducted in the taxing jurisdiction
- National tax identification number, if such a number is issued to the supplier in the supplier's jurisdiction to conduct business in that jurisdiction.

3.139   The simplest way to engage with tax administrations from a remote location is most likely by electronic processes. An on-line registration application could be made accessible on the home page of the tax administration's web site, preferably available in the languages of the jurisdiction's major trading partners.

C.3.3.2. Input tax recovery – Refunds

3.140   It is reasonable for taxing jurisdictions to limit the scope of a simplified registration and compliance regime to the collection of VAT on business-to-consumer supplies of services and intangibles by non-resident suppliers without making the recovery of input tax available under the simplified regime. Where applicable, the input tax recovery could then remain available for non-resident suppliers under the normal VAT refund or registration and compliance procedure.

C.3.3.3. Return procedure

3.141   As requirements differ widely among jurisdictions, satisfying obligations to file tax returns in multiple jurisdictions is a complex process that often results in considerable compliance burdens for non-resident suppliers. Tax administrations could consider authorising non-resident businesses to file simplified returns, which would be less detailed than returns required for local businesses that are entitled to input tax credits. In establishing the requirements for information under such a simplified approach, it is desirable to strike a balance between the businesses' need for simplicity and the tax administrations' need to verify whether tax obligations have been correctly fulfilled. This information could be confined to:

- Supplier's registration identification number
- Tax period
- Currency and, where relevant, exchange rate used
- Taxable amount at the standard rate
- Taxable amount at reduced rate(s), if any
- Total tax amount payable.

3.142   The option to file electronically in a simple and commonly used format will be essential to facilitating compliance. Many tax administrations have already introduced or are introducing options to submit tax returns electronically.

C.3.3.4. Payments

3.143   The use of electronic payment methods is recommended, allowing non-resident suppliers to remit the tax due electronically. This not only reduces the burden and the cost of the payment process for the supplier, but it also reduces payment processing costs for tax administrations. Jurisdictions could consider accepting payments in the currencies of their main trading partners.

C.3.3.5. Record keeping

3.144   Tax administrations must be able to review data to ensure that the tax has been charged and accounted for correctly. Jurisdictions are encouraged to allow the use of electronic record keeping systems, as business processes have become increasingly automated and paper documents generally have been replaced by documents in an electronic format. Jurisdictions could consider limiting the data to be recorded to what is required to satisfy themselves that the tax for each supply has been charged and accounted for correctly and relying as much as possible on information that is available to suppliers in the course of their normal business activity. This could include the type of supply, the date of the supply, the VAT payable and the information used to determine the place where the customer has its usual residence. Taxing jurisdictions could require these records to be made available on request within a reasonable delay.

C.3.3.6. Invoicing

3.145   Invoicing requirements for VAT purposes are among the most burdensome responsibilities of VAT systems. Jurisdictions could therefore consider eliminating invoice requirements for business-to-consumer supplies that are covered by the simplified registration and compliance regime, in light of the fact that the customers involved generally will not be entitled to deduct the input VAT paid on these supplies.

3.146   If invoices are required, jurisdictions could consider allowing invoices to be issued in accordance with the rules of the supplier's jurisdiction or accepting commercial documentation that is issued for purposes other than VAT (e.g. electronic receipts). It is recommended that information on the invoice remain limited to the data required to administer the VAT regime (such as the identification of the customer, type and date of the supply(ies), the taxable amount and VAT amount per VAT rate and the total taxable amount). Jurisdictions could consider allowing this invoice to be submitted in the languages of their main trading partners.

C.3.3.7. Availability of information

3.147   Jurisdictions are encouraged to make available on-line all information necessary to register and comply with the simplified registration and compliance regime, preferably in the languages of their major trading partners. Jurisdictions are also encouraged to make accessible via the Internet the relevant and up-to-date information that non-resident businesses are likely to need in making their tax determinations. In particular, this would include information on tax rates and product classification.

C.3.3.8. Use of third-party service providers

3.148   Compliance for non-resident suppliers could be further facilitated by allowing such suppliers to appoint a third-party service provider to act on their behalf in carrying out certain procedures, such as submitting returns. This could be especially helpful for small and medium enterprises and businesses that are faced with multi-jurisdictional obligations.

C.3.3.9. Application in a business-to-business context

3.149   The implementation of a simplified registration and compliance regime for non-resident suppliers is recommended primarily in the context of business-to-consumer supplies of services and intangibles by non-resident suppliers. These Guidelines recommend the reverse charge mechanism for cross-border business-to-business supplies of services and intangibles that are taxable in the jurisdiction where the customer is located in accordance with Guideline 3.2. If the customer is entitled to full input tax credit in respect of this supply, it could be that the local VAT legislation does not require the reverse charge to be made. Jurisdictions whose general rules do not differentiate between business-to-business and business-to-consumers supplies in their national legislation may consider allowing the use of the simplified registration and compliance regime for both types of supplies.

C.3.3.10. Proportionality

3.150   Jurisdictions should aim to implement a registration-based collection mechanism for business-to-consumer supplies of services and intangibles by non-resident suppliers, without creating compliance and administrative burdens that are disproportionate to the revenues involved or to the objective of achieving neutrality between domestic and foreign suppliers (see also Guideline 2.6).

3.151   This objective should be pursued primarily through the implementation of simplified registration and compliance mechanisms that are consistent across jurisdictions and that are sufficiently clear and accessible to allow easy compliance by non-resident suppliers, notably by small and medium enterprises. Some jurisdictions have implemented a threshold of supplies into the jurisdiction of taxation below which non-resident suppliers would be relieved of the obligation to collect and remit tax in that jurisdiction, with a view to further reducing compliance costs. Relieving suppliers of the obligation to register in jurisdictions where their sales are minimal in value may not lead to substantial net losses of revenue in light of the offsetting expenses of tax administration. The introduction of thresholds needs to be considered carefully. A balance will need to be struck between minimising compliance burdens for non-resident suppliers and costs of tax administration while ensuring that resident businesses are not placed at a competitive disadvantage.

C.3.4. International co-operation to support VAT collection in cases where the supplier is not located in the jurisdiction of taxation

3.152   While simplification is a key means of enhancing compliance by non-resident suppliers with a registration-based collection mechanism for cross-border business-to-consumer supplies of services and intangibles, it is necessary to reinforce taxing authorities' enforcement capacity through enhanced international co-operation in tax administration in the field of indirect taxes.

3.153   Improved international co-operation could focus on the exchange of information and on assistance in recovery. Mutual administrative assistance is a key means to achieve the proper collection and remittance of the tax on cross-border supplies of services and intangibles by non-resident suppliers. It will also be helpful in identifying suppliers, verifying the status of customers, monitoring the volume of supplies, and ensuring that the proper amount of tax is charged. The exchange of information between the tax authorities of the jurisdictions of supply and consumption has a key role to play. This could include the use of spontaneous exchanges of information.

3.154   Chapter 4, Section B of these Guidelines describes the principal existing OECD instruments for exchange of information and other forms of mutual administrative assistance that can assist jurisdictions in strengthening the international administrative co-operation in the field of indirect taxes. These Guidelines recommend that jurisdictions take appropriate steps towards making greater use of these and other available legal instruments for international administrative co-operation to ensure the effective collection of VAT on cross-border business-to-consumer supplies of services and intangibles by non-resident businesses. Such co-operation could be enhanced through the development of a common standard for the exchange of information that is simple, minimises the costs for tax administrations and businesses by limiting the amount of data that is exchanged, and which can be implemented in a short timeframe. Against this background, the OECD's Committee on Fiscal Affairs (CFA) intends to conduct work on further, detailed guidance for the effective exchange of information and other forms of mutual assistance between tax authorities in the field of indirect taxes.

D. Business-to-business and business-to-consumer supplies – Specific rules

D.1. Evaluation framework for assessing the desirability of a specific rule

---

Guideline 3.7

The taxing rights over internationally traded services or intangibles supplied between businesses may be allocated by reference to a proxy other than the customer's location as laid down in Guideline 3.2, when both the following conditions are met:

The allocation of taxing rights by reference to the customer's location does not lead to an appropriate result when considered under the following criteria:

- Neutrality
- Efficiency of compliance and administration
- Certainty and simplicity
- Effectiveness
- Fairness.

A proxy other than the customer's location would lead to a significantly better result when considered under the same criteria.

Similarly, the taxing rights over internationally traded business-to-consumer supplies of services or intangibles may be allocated by reference to a proxy other than the place of performance as laid down in Guideline 3.5 and the usual residence of the customer as laid down in Guideline 3.6, when both the conditions are met as set out in a. and b. above.

3.155   According to Guideline 3.2, the jurisdiction where the customer is located has the taxing rights over services or intangibles supplied across international borders in a business-to-business context. This is the general rule for determining the place of taxation for business-to-business supplies of services and intangibles. In a business-to-consumer context, two general rules are set out in Guidelines 3.5 and 3.6 respectively for two main types of supplies of services and intangibles:

- According to Guideline 3.5, the jurisdiction in which the supply is physically performed has the taxing rights over business-to-consumer on-the-spot supplies of services and intangibles.[38]

- According to Guideline 3.6, the jurisdiction in which the customer has its usual residence has the taxing rights over business-to-consumer supplies of services and intangibles other than those covered by Guideline 3.5.

3.156   It is recognised that these general rules might not give an appropriate tax result in every situation and, where this is the case, the allocation of taxing rights by reference to another proxy might be justified. A rule that allocates taxing rights using a proxy other than those recommended by Guideline 3.2 (for business-to-business supplies) or Guidelines 3.5 and 3.6 (for business-to consumer supplies), is referred to in these Guidelines as a "specific rule". Such a rule will use a different proxy (e.g. location of movable or immovable tangible property, actual location of the customer, or place of effective use and enjoyment) to determine which jurisdiction has the taxing rights over a supply of a service or intangible that is covered by the rule. Any such specific rule should be supported by clear criteria and its application should remain limited. Guideline 3.7 describes these criteria and sets out how they may justify the implementation of a specific rule.

3.157   Under Guideline 3.7, a two-step approach is recommended to determine whether a specific rule is justified:

- The first step is to test whether the relevant general rule leads to an appropriate result under the criteria set out under Guideline 3.7. Where this is the case, there is no need for a specific rule. Where the analysis suggests that the relevant general rule would not lead to an appropriate result, the use of a specific rule might be justified. In such case, a second step is required.

- The second step is to test the proposed specific rule against the criteria of Guideline 3.7. The use of a specific rule will be justified only when this analysis suggests that it would lead to a significantly better result than the use of the relevant general rule.

3.158   These Guidelines do not aim to identify the types of supplies of services or intangibles, nor the particular circumstances or factors, for which a specific rule might be justified. Rather, they provide an evaluation framework for jurisdictions to assess the desirability of a specific rule against the background of a constantly changing technological and commercial environment. The next paragraphs describe this framework in further detail.

---

38. On-the-spot supplies are services and intangibles that are normally physically performed at a readily identifiable location and that are ordinarily consumed at the same time and place where they are physically performed, in the presence of both the person performing the supply and the person consuming it (see para. 3.116).

3.159   The evaluation framework for assessing the desirability of a specific rule builds on the overall objective of the Guidelines on place of taxation, as described in paragraph 3.3. In accordance with this objective, the evaluation framework for assessing the desirability of a specific rule on place of taxation consists of the following criteria:

- Neutrality: The six Guidelines on neutrality and their comments (Guidelines 2.1 to 2.6).

- Efficiency of compliance and administration: Compliance costs for taxpayers and administrative costs for the tax authorities should be minimised as far as possible.

- Certainty and simplicity: The tax rules should be clear and simple to understand so that taxpayers can anticipate the tax consequences in advance of a transaction, including knowing when, where and how to account for the tax.

- Effectiveness: The tax rules should produce the right amount of tax at the right time and the right place.

- Fairness: The potential for tax evasion and avoidance should be minimised while keeping counteractive measures proportionate to the risks involved.

3.160   Ensuring that the tax treatment of internationally traded supplies is in accordance with these criteria requires a consistent definition and implementation of place of taxation rules. The general rules in Guidelines 3.2, 3.5 and 3.6 set out recommended approaches for ensuring a consistent determination of place of taxation for internationally traded services and intangibles. The use of specific rules that use different proxies from these main approaches should be limited to the greatest possible extent, since the existence of specific rules will increase the risk of differences in interpretation and application between jurisdictions and thereby increase the risks of double taxation and unintended non-taxation.[39]

3.161   When assessing the desirability of a specific rule on the basis of the evaluation framework set out above, one should consider each of the criteria while also recognising that they form a package. No single criterion can be considered in isolation as the criteria are all interconnected. For example, neutrality, as described in the Guidelines on neutrality, and efficiency of compliance and administration are complementary to one another. Similarly, efficiency depends on the degree of certainty and simplicity, whereas certainty

---

39. This should not be taken to suggest that countries must change their law to literally incorporate Guidelines 3.2, 3.5 and 3.6 as legal rules in national legislation. Rather, these Guidelines recommend what should be the end result of the national place of taxation rules, however they are described in the relevant laws, without predicting precisely by which means that result is achieved.

and simplicity are also fundamental to achieving effectiveness and fairness. It is therefore unlikely that evaluating the performance of a general rule (or an alternative specific rule) in a particular scenario would result in a very low ranking when judged against one or two criteria but in a much higher ranking when judged against the other criteria. Rather, it is expected that the evaluation will reveal either a good or a poor outcome overall.

3.162   Consequently, it is recommended that jurisdictions consider implementing a specific rule for the allocation of taxing rights on internationally traded services and intangibles only if the overall outcome of the evaluation on the basis of the criteria set out in Guideline 3.7 suggests that the relevant general rule would not lead to an appropriate result and an evaluation on the basis of the same criteria suggests that the proposed specific rule would lead to a significantly better result.

3.163   While there remains a level of subjectivity as to what is and what is not an "appropriate result" and what is "a significantly better result", Guideline 3.7 provides a framework for assessing the desirability of a specific rule that should make the adoption of such a rule more transparent, systematic and verifiable. It is neither feasible nor desirable to provide more prescriptive instructions on what should be the outcome of the evaluation for all supplies of services and intangibles. However, the paragraphs below provide further guidance and specific considerations for particular supplies of services and intangibles for which a specific rule might be appropriate in some circumstances and conditions. The evaluation should be considered from the perspective of both businesses and tax administrations.

D.2. Circumstances where a specific rule may be desirable

3.164   It is recognised that the general rules on place of taxation as set out in Guideline 3.2, for business-to-business supplies, and in Guidelines 3.5 and 3.6, for business-to-consumer supplies, will lead to an appropriate result when considered against the criteria set out in Guideline 3.7 in most circumstances. However, the following paragraphs describe a number of specific circumstances where jurisdictions might find that the application of these general rules is likely to lead to an inappropriate result when considered against these criteria and that a specific rule might lead to a significantly better result.

D.2.1. Examples of circumstances where a specific rule might be desirable in a business-to-business context

3.165   In a business-to-business context, the general rule based on the customer's location might not lead to an appropriate result when considered against the criteria of Guideline 3.7 and a specific rule could lead to a significantly better result in situations where all the following circumstances are met:

- particular services or intangibles are typically supplied to both businesses and final consumers,
- the service requires, in some way, the physical presence of both the person providing the supply and the person receiving the supply, and
- the service is used at a readily identifiable location.

3.166   If businesses that usually supply services or intangibles to a large number of customers for relatively small amounts in a short period of time (e.g. restaurant services) were required to follow the general rule based on the customer's location for business-to-business supplies, it would impose a significant compliance burden on suppliers. Any customer, business or non-business, could simply state that it was a business located in another country and request that no VAT be charged. It would put the supplier at considerable risk of having to bear the under-declared tax if it was subsequently shown that the customer was not a business located in another country (breach of certainty and simplicity). This would also make tax administration controls more difficult as evidence of location might be difficult to produce (breach of efficiency). The same considerations could apply to services that consist of granting the right to access events such as a concert, a sports game, or even a trade fair or exhibition that is designed primarily for businesses. If a ticket can be purchased at the entrance of the building where the event takes place, businesses as well as final consumers can be recipients of the service. In these cases, under the general rule based on the customer's location for business-to-business supplies, the supplier is confronted with the difficulty and risk of identifying and providing evidence of the customer's status and location. Efficiency, as well as certainty and simplicity, might then not be met. Fairness could be at risk. The adoption of a specific rule allocating the taxing rights to the jurisdiction where the event takes place could lead to a significantly better result when considered against the criteria of Guideline 3.7. In such circumstances, jurisdictions might consider using a proxy based on the place of physical performance, which would apply both for business-to-business supplies and business-to-consumer supplies (see Guideline 3.5).

D.2.2. *Examples of circumstances where a specific rule might be desirable in a business-to-consumer context*

3.167   In a business-to-consumer context, jurisdictions might find that the general rules set out in Guidelines 3.5 and 3.6 do not lead to an appropriate result when considered against the criteria of Guideline 3.7 in certain specific circumstances, where they lead to an allocation of taxing rights that is inefficient and overly burdensome from an administrative standpoint (breach of efficiency and of certainty and simplicity) and/or are not sufficiently accurate in predicting the likely place of final consumption (breach of effectiveness and of neutrality). For example, this might occur in the following circumstances:

- The general rule based on the place of physical performance (Guideline 3.5), in respect of on-the-spot supplies of services and intangibles, might not lead to an appropriate result when considered against the criteria of Guideline 3.7 in cases where the physical performance occurs in multiple jurisdictions because tax obligations could arise in multiple jurisdictions (breach of the efficiency and the certainty and simplicity requirements). An example is the international transport of persons.

- In cases where consumption is most likely to occur somewhere other than in the customer's usual place of residence, the general rule based on the place of the usual residence of the customer for supplies of services and intangibles not covered by Guideline 3.5 (Guideline 3.6) might not be sufficiently accurate in predicting the place of final consumption (breach of the effectiveness and the neutrality requirements). Examples could include services and intangibles that are performed at a readily identifiable location and that require the physical presence of the person consuming the supply but not the physical presence of the person performing it, such as the provision of Internet access in an Internet café or a hotel lobby, the use of a telephone booth to make a phone call or the access to television channels for a fee in a hotel room.[40] In such cases, it is reasonable to assume that suppliers will know or are capable of knowing the actual location of the customer at the likely time of consumption and jurisdictions may then consider using the actual location of the consumer at the time of the supply as a proxy for place of consumption.

D.3. Special considerations for supplies of services and intangibles directly connected with tangible property

3.168   Jurisdictions often choose to rely on the location of tangible property for determining the place of taxation for supplies of services and intangibles connected with tangible property or with the supply of such property. The business use or final consumption of such services is then considered to be so connected with the business use or the final consumption of the tangible property that the location of this tangible property is considered as the most appropriate place of taxation.

---

40. The supplies in these examples are performed at a readily identifiable location and require the physical presence of the person consuming the supply but they do not require the physical presence of the person performing them. These are therefore not "on-the-spot" supplies covered by Guideline 3.5 and their place of taxation is in principle determined by reference to the customer's usual residence, in accordance with Guideline 3.6.

3.169   The following sections look specifically at services and intangibles connected with immovable property, as this is a particularly complex area where a specific rule is already applied by many jurisdictions both in a business-to-business context and in a business-to-consumer context (Sections D.3.1-D.3.4). This is complemented by a section on services and intangibles connected with movable tangible property, which explains that a rule based on the location of the movable tangible property might be particularly appropriate for identifying the place of taxation in a business-to-consumer context (Section D.3.5).

D.3.1. Specific rule for supplies of services and intangibles directly connected with immovable property

---

Guideline 3.8

For internationally traded supplies of services and intangibles directly connected with immovable property, the taxing rights may be allocated to the jurisdiction where the immovable property is located.

3.170   According to this specific rule, taxing rights are allocated to the jurisdiction where the immovable property is located.

3.171   This Guideline does not list particular supplies of services and intangibles that may or may not fall under such a specific rule. Instead, it identifies their common features and establishes categories of supplies of services and intangibles for which the conditions set out in Guideline 3.7 might be met and for which implementation of such a specific rule might therefore be justified.

D.3.2. Circumstances where a specific rule for supplies of services and intangibles directly connected with immovable property might be appropriate

3.172   When internationally traded services and intangibles are directly connected with immovable property, there may be circumstances where a specific rule allocating the taxing rights to the jurisdiction where the immovable property is located might be appropriate.

3.173   This is most likely to be the case when there is a supply of services or intangibles falling within one of the following categories:

- the transfer, sale, lease or the right to use, occupy, enjoy or exploit immovable property,

- supplies of services that are physically provided to the immovable property itself, such as constructing, altering and maintaining the immovable property, or

- other supplies of services and intangibles that do not fall within the first two categories but where there is a very close, clear and obvious link or association with the immovable property.

3.174   The second condition for the implementation of a specific rule under Guideline 3.7 requires that such a specific rule would lead to a significantly better result than the relevant general rule when evaluated against the criteria of Guideline 3.7. While it is reasonable to assume that this second condition is met for the first two categories of supplies identified above, its fulfilment for the supplies mentioned in the last category above is likely to require an evaluation as set out in Guideline 3.7 before the implementation of a specific rule can be considered.

D.3.3. Common features of supplies of services and intangibles directly connected with immovable property

3.175   The supplies of services and intangibles for which Guideline 3.8 may apply are referred to as "services directly connected with immovable property". This expression does not have an independent meaning but aims simply to narrow the scope of the specific rule in the sense that it contemplates that there should be a very close, clear and obvious link or association between the supply and the immovable property. This very close, clear and obvious link or association is considered to exist only when the immovable property is clearly identifiable.

3.176   For the supply to be considered as directly connected with immovable property, it is not sufficient that a connection with immovable property be merely one aspect of the supply among many others: the connection with immovable property must be at the heart of the supply and must constitute its predominant characteristic. This is particularly relevant with respect to composite supplies involving immovable property. If a connection with immovable property is only one part of the supply, this will not be sufficient for the supply to fall under one of the three categories.

D.3.4. Further description of the supplies of services and intangibles directly connected with immovable property for which a specific rule might be appropriate

3.177   The transfer, sale, lease, or the right to use, occupy, enjoy or exploit immovable property, encompasses all kinds of utilisation of immovable property, i.e. supplies of services and intangibles "derived from" the immovable property (as opposed to other circumstances where the supplies are directed to the immovable property). The terms "transfer", "sale", "lease", and "right to use, occupy, enjoy or exploit" therefore should not be understood narrowly within the meaning of national civil laws. It should be noted however, that these supplies fall under this Guideline only when they are considered to be supplies of services or intangibles under national law, i.e. when they are not considered to be supplies of goods or of immovable property.[41]

3.178   Supplies of services such as the construction, alteration and maintenance of immovable property cover services that are typically physical in nature, as opposed, for example, to intellectual services. Such supplies of services are physically provided to immovable property. These are services that aim to change or maintain the physical status of the immovable property. Typical cases in practice will include, for example, the construction of a building[42] as well as its renovation or demolition, the painting of a building or even the cleaning of it (inside or outside).

3.179   In addition to the utilisation of immovable property and services that are physically performed on immovable property, there might be other supplies of services and intangibles where there is a very close, clear and obvious link or association with immovable property and where taxation in the jurisdiction of the immovable property leads to a significantly better result than the relevant general rule when considered under the criteria defined in Guideline 3.7. When considering the adoption of a specific rule, jurisdictions may in particular wish to take into account, in addition to the requirement of a very close, clear and obvious link or association between the supply and the immovable property, whether such a specific rule has a sufficiently high potential to be manageable and enforceable in practice. For example, certain intellectual services,[43] such as architectural services that relate to clearly identifiable, specific immovable property, could be considered to have a sufficiently close connection with immovable property.

D.3.5. *Services and intangibles connected with movable tangible property*

3.180   Examples of services and intangibles connected with movable property include services that are physically carried out on specific movable property such as repairing, altering or maintaining the property, and the rental of specific movable property where this is considered a service. Jurisdictions might consider implementing an approach based on the location of movable

---

41. Other rules will be applicable to such supplies, although they might lead to the same result.
42. If this is not treated as a supply of goods or of immovable property, for which other rules might apply, although they could lead to the same result.
43. The adjective "intellectual" has a broad meaning and is not limited to regulated professions.

tangible property for identifying the place of taxation of such supplies of services and intangibles connected with movable tangible property. Such an approach ensures that the place of taxation rules for such supplies provide a reasonably accurate reflection of the place where the consumption of the services or intangibles is likely to take place and is relatively straightforward for suppliers to apply in practice, particularly in the case of business-to-consumer supplies. Services or intangibles connected with movable tangible property supplied to final consumers, such as repair services, will generally be consumed in the jurisdiction where the property is located. Movable tangible property that is shipped abroad after the service is performed will generally be subject to import VAT under standard customs rules when crossing the customs border. This ensures that the taxing rights accrue to the jurisdiction of consumption when the tangible property moves across the customs border. Jurisdictions generally complement these rules by giving temporary VAT relief in the jurisdiction where the supply is performed and where the movable property is temporarily located, if this property is subsequently exported. This treatment lies outside the scope of these Guidelines.[44]

3.181   For business-to-business supplies of services and intangibles connected with movable property, the application of the general rule based on the customer's location will generally lead to an appropriate result.

---

44. Also the treatment of services that are incidental to the export or import of goods (e.g. packaging, loading, transport, insurance etc.) is outside the scope of these Guidelines.

ANNEX I TO CHAPTER 3

Examples to illustrate the application of the general rule on place of taxation for business-to-business supplies of services and intangibles to single location entities

The examples in this annex are illustrative of the principles set out in the Guidelines and consequently are not intended to be exhaustive. The place of taxation of internationally traded services and intangibles will be determined according to the facts of each individual supply.

Example 1: Supply between 2 separate legal entities (whether related by common ownership or not)

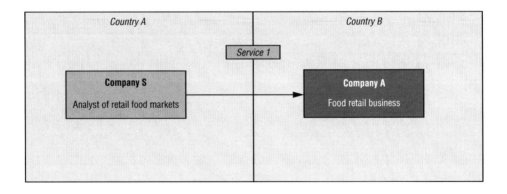

Facts

Company S is a business located in Country A specialising in analysing retail food markets, Company A is a food retail business located in Country B. Neither Company S nor Company A has other establishments for VAT purposes.

Company A is considering expanding its retailing activities beyond Country B and approaches Company S. The two companies enter into a business agreement under which Company S will provide an analysis of market conditions in Country A to Company A. Company A will pay Company S a sum of money in return for Company S performing its obligations under this business agreement.

Place of taxation

According to the business agreement, Company S will be the supplier and Company B will be the customer. There will be a supply of a service provided by the supplier to the customer for consideration. In accordance with the general rule for business-to-business supplies (Guideline 3.2), the place of taxation will be Country B, which is the country where the customer is located.

The result remains the same even where the supplier and customer are two separate legal entities related by ownership.

Example 2: Two separate supplies involving three separate legal entities

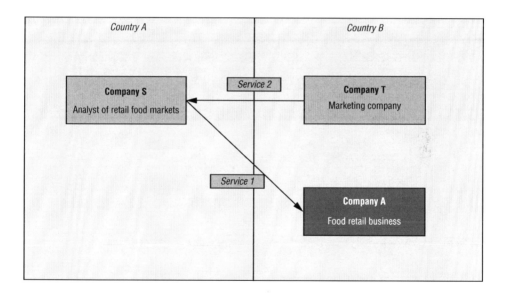

Facts

As Company A subsequently requested Company S to also perform studies on its own market in Country B, Company S engages the services of a marketing company in Country B, Company T. This company has no ownership connection with Company S or Company A.

Company T supplies its services of marketing to Company S under a business agreement (Service 2). The supply of Service 1 between Company S and Company A (as outlined in Example 1 – analysis of the market conditions in Country A) continues as before.

Place of taxation

According to the business agreement Company T is the supplier and Company S the customer. There is a supply of services for consideration. Therefore, in accordance with the general rule for business-to-business supplies (Guideline 3.2), the supply by Company T will be subject to taxation in Country A because that is the country where the customer is located. These are two independent supplies and are treated accordingly.

The outcome of Service 1 as outlined in Example 1 remains unaffected.

Example 3: A global agreement

This example illustrates the supplies that occur when a global agreement for a supply of auditing services is entered into between the parent company of an audit group and a centralised purchasing company of the group requiring audit services for other group members in various countries.

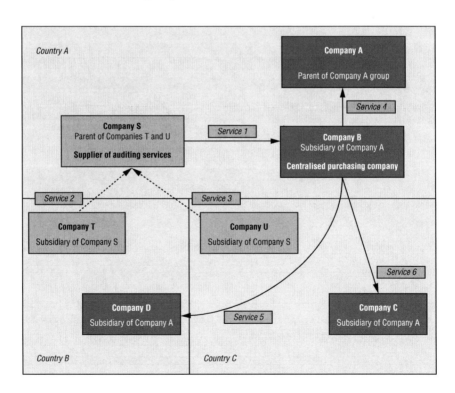

Facts

Company B is a centralised purchasing company in Country A. It belongs to a multinational company group with subsidiaries around the world, notably Company D in Country B and Company C in Country C. The parent company of Company B is Company A, also located in Country A.

Company S in Country A is the parent company of a multinational auditing company group with subsidiaries around the world, notably Company T in Country B and Company U in Country C.

Company A Group requires a global auditing service to meet legal requirements for the companies in Country A and its subsidiaries in Countries B and C. The global auditing service is purchased for the whole group by Company B, which therefore concludes a centralised purchasing agreement with Company S to supply auditing services to the whole Company A Group. Payment will follow each business agreement.

The global auditing service is supplied by Company S to Company B in return for consideration. While this service includes the supply of all components of the global agreement, Company S is able to actually perform only part of the services itself, namely the services to Companies A and B that are located in Country A. To be able to fulfil the rest of the agreement, Company S enters into business agreements with its two subsidiaries, Company T and Company U, under which these companies supply auditing services to their parent Company S. Companies S and T provide these services directly to the subsidiaries of Company A. These subsidiaries, Companies C and D, are in the same countries as the subsidiaries of Company A that provide the auditing service to them.

Company B enters into separate business agreements with its parent Company A and Company A's subsidiaries C and D. Under these business agreements, Company B supplies the auditing services that it has acquired from Company S, to Company A and to Company A's subsidiaries C and D.

There are six separate business agreements in this example, each leading to a supply of a service for consideration:

- Company S is the supplier and Company B is the customer under the centralised purchase agreement (Service 1).
- Companies T and U are the suppliers and Company S is the customer under two different business agreements (Service 2 and Service 3).
- Company B is the supplier and Company A is the customer under a different agreement (Service 4).
- Company B is the supplier and Company D and Company C are the customers under two different business agreements (Service 5 and Service 6).

The place of taxation will be decided for each supply individually.

Place of taxation

In accordance with the general rule for business-to-business supplies (Guideline 3.2), the place of taxation for the supply of Service 1 between Company S and Company B will be Country A as Company B is in Country A. In accordance with the general rule for business-to-business supplies (Guideline 3.2), the place of taxation for the supply of Services 2 and 3 between Company T and Company U as suppliers and Company S as a customer is Country A for both supplies. In accordance with the general rule for business-to-business supplies (Guideline 3.2) the place of taxation for the supply of Service 4 between Company B and Company A will be Country A as Company A is in Country A. In accordance with the general rule for business-to-business supplies (Guideline 3.2), the place of taxation for the supply of Service 5 between Company B and Company D will be Country B because Country B is the country where the customer is located. In accordance with the general rule for business-to-business supplies (Guideline 3.2), the place of taxation for the supply of Service 6 between Company B and Company C will be Country C because Country C is the country where the customer is located.

It should be noted that the auditing services by Company T and Company U are "supplied to" Company S, while they are "provided" directly to Company D and Company C. The fact that the services are *"supplied to"* someone different from those to which the services are directly "provided" is not relevant in this example to determine the place of taxation, as the place of taxation will still be the customer location as determined in accordance with the general rule for business-to-business supplies (Guideline 3.2) and not where or to whom the services are directly provided.

The reason for this is that, at each stage of this example, all supplies will be subject to the taxation rules in the jurisdiction where the customer is located and the services are deemed to be used by the business in accordance with the destination principle as implemented by the general rule for business-to-business supplies (Guideline 3.2). There is neither double taxation nor unintended non-taxation in Countries A, B and C. In particular, the tax that accrues to Countries B and C reflects the business use of the services in those countries in accordance with the general rule for business-to-business supplies (Guideline 3.2) that treats customer location as the appropriate proxy for the jurisdiction of business use thereby implementing the destination principle. There is no reason to depart from the business agreements e.g. by following the interaction between Company T and Company D or between Company U and Company C.

In developing this example, care has been taken to avoid any "stewardship" issues that may exist with respect to Company A.[45] Company A, as the parent, may also be seen as deriving an element of benefit from the audit activities in Countries A, B and C, for example because such audit included an additional review of financial statements under the parent company's country accounting standards, rather than only per local subsidiary country accounting standards. Stewardship issues are assumed not to arise in Example 3 due to the inclusion of Service 4, where Company B supplies auditing services to Company A. Further, any questions concerning valuation for VAT/GST purposes and the possible identification of supplies existing, other than those shown, are also ignored.

Example 4: Alternative global agreement – Framework agreement

In this example the parent company of the group requiring audit services enters into a global agreement described as a "framework agreement" with the parent company of the audit group (both in the same country) in order to provide audit services in a number of countries.[46]

Facts

Company A is a parent company in Country A. It belongs to a multinational company group with subsidiaries around the world, for example Company B in Country B and Company C in Country C.

Company S is a parent company in Country A belonging to a multinational auditing company group with subsidiaries around the world, for example Company T in Country B and Company U in Country C.

Company A Group requires a global auditing service to meet legal requirements for its companies in Country A and its subsidiaries in Countries B and C. Company A concludes a framework agreement with Company S (Agreement 1). The framework agreement covers definitions, obligations relating to confidentiality, warranties, due dates for payment and limitations of liability, that would only apply if and when members of Company S and Company A enter into separate agreements referring to this framework agreement. The agreement also

---

45. Stewardship expenses are broadly the costs incurred by the parent company of the group for administrative and other services provided to subsidiaries and other affiliates for the benefit of the parent, as a shareholder, rather than for the individual benefit of the subsidiary or affiliate. These costs can be incurred directly by the parent or by the subsidiary and passed on to the parent. Typically, these are treated as expenses which ought to be absorbed by the parent company because they must be regarded as stewardship or shareholders' expenses benefiting the shareholders or the group as a whole and not a subsidiary or affiliate individually.
46. The expression "framework agreement" is used solely to distinguish it from the separate business agreement for audit services to the parent trading company. The Guidelines do not attempt to define in any way what a "framework agreement" might be.

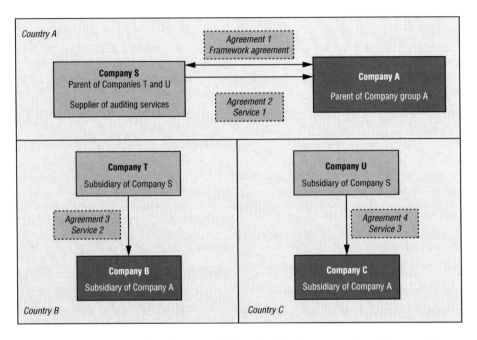

provides that companies that are affiliated with Company A and the auditing companies that are affiliated with Company S may enter into business agreements that will incorporate the terms of the framework agreement by reference. The agreement, however, does not oblige any member of Company A Group or Company S Group to enter into such business agreements.

Company A enters into a separate business agreement with Company S for the audit of Company A (Agreement 2); Company B enters into a business agreement with Company T for the audit of Company B (Agreement 3); and Company C enters into a business agreement with Company U for the audit of Company C (Agreement 4). In each of these three separate agreements (i.e. Agreements 2-4), an article is included where the parties agree to incorporate the terms included in the framework agreement (Agreement 1). Payment will follow each business agreement.

There are four separate agreements in this example, only three of which constitute business agreements that lead to supplies of services for consideration:

● Agreement 1 is not transactional, has no consideration and does not create a supply. Agreement 1 stipulates terms and conditions that become activated only when parties agree to separate business agreements as specified in the framework agreement.

● Under Agreement 2, Company S is the supplier and Company A is the customer (Service 1).

- Under Agreement 3, Company T is the supplier and Company B is the customer (Service 2).
- Under Agreement 4, Company U is the supplier and Company C is the customer (Service 3).

The place of taxation will be decided for each supply individually.

Place of taxation

In accordance with the general rule for business-to-business supplies (Guideline 3.2), the place of taxation for the supply of Service 1 between Company S and Company A will be Country A as Company A is in Country A. In accordance with the general rule for business-to-business supplies (Guideline 3.2), the place of taxation for the supply of Service 2 between Company T and Company U will be Country B as Company B is in Country B. Further, and again in accordance with the general rule for business-to- business supplies (Guideline 3.2), the place of taxation for the supply of Service 3 between Company U and Company C will be Country C as Company C is in Country C.

All three supplies are subject to the taxation rules in the jurisdiction where the customer is located and is the appropriate proxy for the jurisdiction of business use under the general rule for business-to-business supplies (Guideline 3.2). There is neither double taxation nor unintended non-taxation in Countries A, B or C. There is no reason to depart from the business agreements. In particular, no supplies take place under the framework agreement (Agreement 1) itself in this example. Consequently, no supplies are made under that agreement and no place of taxation issue arises.

Example 5: Alternative global agreement – Different flow of payments

This example expands upon example 4 by introducing payment flows that are different from the flows of the services as set out in the underlying business agreement.

Facts

This example is similar to Example 4 except that the Company A group has put in place a system for settling inter-company supplies between group members. As a result, the Company A group decides to reduce the costs associated with cash disbursements by appointing Company A as the common paymaster for the group.[47] The framework agreement in this example is similar to Example 4 except that it specifies that the payments for the services supplied under the

---

47. It is recognised that, in some cases, the paymaster function could create a separate supply, or supplies, between Company A and its subsidiaries. For the purposes of this example this is not the case.

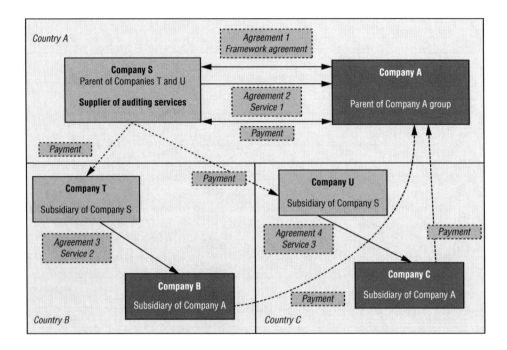

locally concluded business agreements will be handled by Company A directly with Company S for the whole Company A group.

For the audit services supplied under the three business agreements Company S, Company T and Company U will follow the general invoicing process and issue invoices respectively to Company A, Company B and Company C. For payment purposes, however, Company S will issue a collective statement (with copies attached of the invoices issued for the services supplied) to Company A. Based on the collective statement Company A will pay the requested amount to Company S and will on the same day collect the respective amounts from Company B and Company C. Similarly, Company S will transfer the respective amounts over to Company T and Company U on the same day it receives the payment from Company A.

The movements of payment are simply cash or account entries. The payment Company A makes to Company S represents consideration for the services supplied from Company S to Company A, from Company T to Company B and from Company U to Company C.

Place of taxation

The conclusions reached in Example 4 about the place of taxation of the supplies made under the business agreements (Agreements 2, 3 and 4) remain valid. The fact that payments are transferred via Company A and Company S has no impact on those conclusions.

All supplies under the business agreements are subject to the taxation rules in the jurisdiction where the customer is located according to the general rule for business-to- business supplies (Guideline 3.2). There is neither double nor unintended non-taxation in Countries A, B or C. There is no reason to depart from the business agreements e.g. by following the cash flows. The cash flows between Company A and its subsidiaries, between Company A and Company S, and between Company S and its subsidiaries are consideration for services supplied under the business agreements but do not in themselves create additional supplies, nor alter the supplies, nor identify the customer or customer location.

ANNEX II TO CHAPTER 3

Example to illustrate the application of the recharge method under the general rule on place of taxation for business-to-business supplies of services and intangibles to multiple location entities

Supply of payroll services

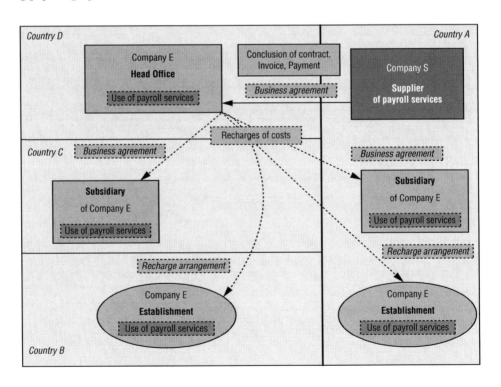

Facts

Company E is a multiple location entity located in three different countries: a head office in Country D ("Head Office") and trading establishments ("Establishments") in Countries A and B. It is the parent company of a multinational group with subsidiaries ("Subsidiaries") in Countries A and C. Company E's Head Office and Establishments as well as its Subsidiaries are all registered for VAT purposes.

Company E, represented by its Head Office, enters into a business agreement with Supplier S, located in Country A, for the supply of payroll management services. In this example, the payroll management services[48] relate to staff of Company E's Head Office and of its Establishments in Countries A and B and its Subsidiaries in Country A and C.

At its Head Office, Company E has business agreements in place with its Subsidiaries and recharge arrangements with its Establishments, setting out the terms and conditions for the transactions between them.

The business agreement between Supplier S and Company E establishes a fixed fee per month if the number of employees is within a given range. The fees for the services supplied under this business agreement are paid to Supplier S by Company E's Head Office on receipt of an invoice from Supplier S.

The agreed fee is 20 000. Supplier S issues an invoice for this amount to the Head Office of Company E, from which it receives payment of the entire amount.

Supplier

Supplier S in Country A has entered into a business agreement with Company E. It was negotiated and concluded for Company E by its Head Office in Country D, to which all invoices are addressed and which is responsible for payment. The business agreement provides the evidence allowing the supplier to supply the service free of VAT and to issue an invoice to Company E's Head Office in Country D without VAT.

Customer group[49]

After having represented Company E in the business agreement with Supplier S, the Head Office of Company E will typically have set up this supplier within the

---

48. Payroll management services include multiple steps such as data collection, master data input in systems, tracking of legislation changes, calculation of taxes, issuance of pay sheets, preparation of accounting entries, preparation of bank transfer files, issue of summary reports, etc.
49. In the context of this example, the term "customer group" refers to Company E and its Establishments and Subsidiaries that employ the staff to which the services supplied by Supplier S relate.

"supplier master data" of its ERP system[50] and will have created a cost centre to capture and pool the relevant costs. In this example, the Head Office has represented Company E in a business agreement to purchase services for its own use and for Company E's Establishments in Countries A and B and its Subsidiaries in Countries A and C. The Head Office of Company E will therefore consider the appropriate methodology for allocating the costs of these services to the Head Office and to its Establishments and Subsidiaries. In this example, the allocation will be based on the number of employees (or "headcount"). In this case headcount presents a fair and reasonable picture of the use of the payroll management services, by Company E's Head Office and its Establishments and Subsidiaries that employ the staff to which these services relate. Headcount is thus considered as an acceptable cost allocation key for these services.

The terms and conditions for the cost allocations to the Establishments and Subsidiaries will be reflected in business agreements between Company E and its Subsidiaries and in the recharge arrangements between the Head Office of Company E and its Establishments.

Upon receipt of the invoice from Supplier S, the accounts payable team in the Head Office of Company E will enter this invoice into the cost centre for invoices that have to be allocated on the basis of headcount for the onward supplies.

Next, the appropriate VAT treatment ("coding") will be assigned to this entry. This is typically based on a "decision tree", considering the various possible VAT scenarios. The conclusion for Company E's Head Office in this case will be that the invoice received from Supplier S should show no VAT and that the Head Office should account for the VAT in Country D under a reverse charge mechanism.[51] Once approved, the invoice will be processed for payment by the Head Office directly to Supplier S and the Head Office will account for the VAT in Country D under a reverse charge mechanism. Company E's Head

---

50. Enterprise resource planning ("ERP") systems integrate internal and external management flows and information across an entire organisation, embracing finance and accounting functions, manufacturing, sales and services, customer relationship management, etc. ERP systems automate this activity with an integrated software application. Their purpose is to facilitate the flow of information between all business functions within an organisation and to manage the connections to outside stakeholders such as suppliers and customers. See Bidgoli, Hossein, (2004). The Internet Encyclopedia, Volume 1, John Wiley & Sons, Inc. p. 707.
51. For the purpose of this example, it is assumed that all countries apply a "reverse charge mechanism" that switches the liability to pay the tax from the supplier to the customer. It is recognised that some countries do not require the customer to account for the tax under the reverse charge mechanism when entitled to full input tax credit.

Office in Country D will deduct the related input tax in line with its normal right to deduct.

Next, the Head Office of Company E will recharge part of the cost of the payroll services to the Establishments and Subsidiaries that employ the staff to which these services relate. This action is usually part of the regular "accounting close" that would for instance be run at the end of each month, quarter, semester or accounting year. In many cases, this will be done on the basis of an "allocation key table" maintained in the accounting software, highlighting for each account or range of accounts the percentage to be used to allocate the amounts that have been identified for recharge earlier in the process. This close out routine will calculate the amount per Establishment and Subsidiary, produce documentation and place the accounting entries.

In this example, the allocation key is based on headcount. The Head Office of Company E will identify the number of employees on payroll in each of the relevant Establishments and Subsidiaries, typically on the basis of budget data. In this example, budget data show that the Head Office employs 100 staff, the Establishments in Countries A and B employ respectively 10 and 30 staff and its Subsidiaries in Countries A and C respectively have 20 and 40 employees.

The allocation key table will attribute 50% to the Head Office in Country D, 5% to the Establishment in Country A, 15% to the Establishment in Country B, 10 % to the Subsidiary in Country A and 20% to the Subsidiary in Country C. The accounting system at the Head Office of Company E will produce two invoices for the onward supply to its Subsidiaries, one for 2 000 to the Subsidiary in Country A and one for 4 000 to the Subsidiary in Country C.[52] Based on the general rule for business-to-business supplies (Guideline 3.2), these invoices will be issued free of VAT since these Subsidiaries are single location entities located outside Country D where the Head Office of Company E is located. The accounting system will also generate two internal documents equivalent to invoices for the allocation of 1 000 to its Establishment in Country A and of 3 000 to its Establishment in Country B. Under the recharge method, these documents will receive the same treatment as if they were invoices to a separate legal entity, and will be issued free of VAT since both Establishments are located outside Country D where the Head Office of Company E is located.

Upon receipt of the invoices, the Subsidiaries in Countries A and C will account for the VAT through the reverse charge. The Establishments in Countries A and B will account for VAT through the reverse charge upon receipt of the documents for the costs allocated to them by their Head Office.

This process will be repeated throughout the accounting year. It may be possible in certain cases that allocation keys would remain unchanged in the course of

---

52. See Section B.4 of Chapter 3.

the accounting year, even if the number of employees by entity would fluctuate during that period. In such a case, companies will typically, at year end, perform a "true up" calculation. The cost allocation will then be reconsidered on the basis of the more precise headcount, taking into account fluctuations in the course of the accounting year. Correcting credit notes or invoices/documents will then be created for the difference between the amount actually charged and the amount as calculated on the basis of actual headcount. These additional invoices or credit notes will follow a VAT treatment similar to the underlying invoices/documents.

Tax administrations

The supplier in Country A should hold all the relevant information that constitutes the business agreement to demonstrate that he has correctly supplied the service free of VAT to Company E's Head Office.

The tax administration in Country D should be able to ensure that the reverse charge is brought to account correctly by Company E's Head Office on the invoice received from Supplier S. It should also be able to ensure a correct tax treatment of the recharges made by Company E's Head Office to its Establishments and Subsidiaries. Company E's Head Office should hold all the relevant information that constitutes the business agreement with Supplier S. It should also hold the business agreements with its Subsidiaries and the recharge arrangements with its Establishments demonstrating how the recharges were allocated.

The tax administrations in Country A, B and C should be able to ensure that the reverse charge is brought to account correctly by the Subsidiaries and Establishments of Company E on the recharges made by the Head Office. The Subsidiaries should hold all the relevant information that constitutes their business agreement with Company E through its Head Office and the Establishments should hold the relevant information that constitutes their recharge arrangement with their Head Office. In particular, the tax administrations in Countries A and B should be able to verify that the Establishments have accounted for tax at the correct time of taxation under the normal domestic rules (e.g. date of internal recharge documents, date consideration is paid to the Head Office).

In order to audit the recharges, the tax administrations will need to be able to see all the relevant commercial documentation down to transaction level in order to identify the nature of the individual service that is recharged and so determine its place of taxation and the applicable rate.

Chapter 4

Supporting the Guidelines in practice mutual co-operation, dispute minimisation, and application in cases of evasion and avoidance

A. Introduction

4.1   The objective of the Guidelines is to provide guidance to jurisdictions in developing practical legislation that will facilitate a smooth interaction between national VAT systems in their application to international trade, with a view to minimising the potential for double taxation and unintended non-taxation and creating more certainty for business and tax authorities. This objective should be achieved principally through adherence to the internationally agreed principles on VAT neutrality set forth in Chapter 2 and through implementation of the principles for determining the place of taxation of cross-border supplies set forth in Chapter 3.

4.2   In an ideal world, achieving the objective of the Guidelines would be simple. The principles on VAT neutrality set forth in Chapter 2 and on allocating VAT taxing rights in both the business-to-business and business-to-consumer contexts set forth in Chapter 3 would be applied consistently to the widest extent possible. A range of adequate relief mechanisms would also be available for businesses that incurred VAT in jurisdictions where they were not located. Furthermore, the parties involved in the cross-border transactions would all be acting in good faith, and all transactions would be legitimate and possess economic substance.

4.3   In practice, however, there might be differences in the way jurisdictions implement or interpret the neutrality or place of taxation principles in the Guidelines (e.g. determining customer status and location). There might also be differences in the way jurisdictions treat the specific facts of particular cross-border transactions (e.g. differences in the characterisation of supplies) and in the interpretation of the domestic rules by parties to a cross-border supply. Where these differences arise, they could lead to double taxation or unintended non-taxation and, in some instances, to disputes.

4.4   In light of the practical recognition that the Guidelines on neutrality and place of taxation will not entirely eliminate the risk of double taxation or unintended non-taxation in the application of VAT to cross-border supplies of services and intangibles, or the disputes that inconsistent interpretation of the Guidelines might engender, it is appropriate to identify other mechanisms that might be available to facilitate the consistent implementation of the principles of the Guidelines in national legislation, as well as their consistent interpretation by tax administrations, in order to minimise both the risk of such double taxation or unintended non-taxation and the potential for resulting disputes.

104

4.5   In addition to the practical issues that can arise in implementing or interpreting the Guidelines when all parties are acting in good faith and all transactions are legitimate and possess economic substance, some cross-border transactions might reflect efforts to evade or avoid taxation, even when national legislation would achieve the objective of the Guidelines for parties engaged in legitimate cross-border transactions with economic substance. In such instances, it is appropriate to recognise that it is not inconsistent with the Guidelines for jurisdictions to take proportionate counter-measures to protect against evasion and avoidance, revenue losses and distortion of competition.

4.6   It is important to emphasise that this Chapter is intended specifically to complement the Guidelines set forth in Chapters 2 and 3. As such, it is directed to concerns of neutrality, place of taxation, and other issues that support the consistent interpretation in practice of these Guidelines, as well as concerns of evasion and avoidance. It is not addressed to concerns outside the scope of the Guidelines in Chapters 2 and 3, such as questions whether a particular jurisdiction should provide concessionary treatment for any particular type of supply (e.g. exemptions or reduced rates) or whether a particular jurisdiction has the right to limit the deductibility of certain input VAT. Nor does it address purely domestic situations without any cross-border aspect. In short, this Chapter focuses essentially on mechanisms for avoiding double taxation and unintended non-taxation, for facilitating the minimisation of disputes over potential double taxation or unintended non-taxation, and for dealing with evasion and avoidance.

4.7   This Chapter is not intended to interfere with the sovereignty of jurisdictions. As in other areas of tax administration, jurisdictions are, however, encouraged to apply the General Administrative Principles approved in 2001 by the OECD Forum on Tax Administration[53] (GAP001 *Principles of Good Tax Administration – Practice Note*), which are reproduced in Chapter 2, Box 2.1.

B. Mutual co-operation, exchange of information, and other arrangements allowing tax administrations to communicate and work together

B.1. Background

4.8   Mechanisms for mutual co-operation, exchange of information and other forms of communication among tax administrations can offer helpful approaches to facilitate a consistent interpretation of the Guidelines on neutrality and on place of taxation, to minimise disputes, and to address issues of evasion or avoidance arising in the context of the Guidelines.

---

53. *www.oecd.org/dataoecd/34/39/1907918.pdf.*

4.9   Because the Guidelines are not legally binding (soft law) these approaches for achieving a consistent interpretation of the Guidelines in national law cannot include any mechanism that depends on the existence of a binding legal commitment (hard law) between countries (e.g. a bilateral tax treaty). For this reason, formal dispute resolution mechanisms cannot constitute mechanisms for producing a consistent interpretation of the Guidelines.

4.10   Jurisdictions nevertheless are encouraged to utilise existing mechanisms for mutual co-operation, information exchange, and mutual assistance, which provide tax administrations with a means of communicating and working together, to facilitate a consistent interpretation under national law or practice of the Guidelines on neutrality and on place of taxation, to facilitate the minimisation of disputes arising within the scope of such Guidelines, and to address issues of evasion and avoidance in the context of the Guidelines.

4.11   Jurisdictions are further encouraged to explore a variety of approaches beyond the existing mechanisms identified immediately below, to effect a consistent interpretation of the Guidelines on neutrality and on place of taxation. These approaches might include the development of additional guidance, under the auspices of the OECD's Committee on Fiscal Affairs (CFA) and its subsidiary bodies, in the form of "best practices" or recommended approaches for implementing the Guidelines as a means of assuring their consistent interpretation.

B.2. Existing mechanisms for mutual co-operation

4.12   The following paragraphs describe the principal existing OECD mechanisms for mutual co-operation, information exchange and other forms of mutual assistance that could assist tax administrations in interpreting and implementing the principles of the Guidelines consistently and thereby minimise the potential for double taxation and unintended non-taxation, as well as disputes that might arise as a result of inconsistent interpretations; they also address questions of evasion and avoidance within the context of the Guidelines. Jurisdictions are also encouraged to use other bilateral, regional or multilateral arrangements that might exist to effect a consistent interpretation of the Guidelines on neutrality and on place of taxation and to address issues of evasion and avoidance in the context of the Guidelines.

B.2.1. Multilateral co-operation

4.13   The *Multilateral Convention on Mutual Administrative Assistance in Tax Matters* (the Convention), which was developed jointly by the OECD and the Council of Europe in 1988 and amended by Protocol in 2010, provides for all possible forms of administrative co-operation between the Parties in the assessment and collection of taxes, in particular with a view to combating tax evasion and avoidance. The Convention has been open to all countries since 2011 and its obligators are subject to any reservation of the Parties. The Convention is intended to have a very wide scope, covering all taxes including general consumption taxes such as the VAT.

B.2.2. Bilateral co-operation

4.14 The *OECD Model Tax Convention* (MTC), while not a binding instrument, deals with exchange of information in Article 26. This provision applies to "such information as is foreseeably relevant … to the administration or enforcement of the domestic laws concerning taxes of every kind and description imposed on behalf of the Contracting States." Its application is not restricted to taxes covered by the Convention, and the provision therefore applies as well to the exchange of information with respect to VAT.

4.15 For countries that have adopted a bilateral tax treaty based on the MTC and an information exchange article based on Article 26, the mechanism appears to offer a promising platform for Parties to exchange information both in individual cases and in broader classes of cases arising under VAT, including cases that raise issues implicating the Guidelines. A bilateral agreement thus provides a possible mechanism for enhanced co-operation and development of solutions to common problems arising under the Guidelines with a view to minimising risks of double taxation and unintended non-taxation.

4.16 The OECD also developed a *Model Agreement on Exchange of Information on Tax Matters* to promote international co-operation in tax matters through exchange of information. This Agreement is not a binding instrument but contains two models for *Tax Information Exchange Agreements* (TIEAs), a multilateral version and a bilateral version. A considerable number of bilateral agreements have been based on this Agreement. These TIEAs provide for exchange of information on request and tax examinations abroad, principally for direct taxes but they can also cover other taxes such as VAT. Furthermore, TIEAs provide for forms of exchange other than exchange on request.

C. Taxpayer services

4.17 In addition to supporting the consistent interpretation of the Guidelines through mutual co-operation, tax administrations might be able to support such consistent interpretation through taxpayer services focused on the Guidelines, when provision of such services is not inconsistent with national law or practice.

4.18 Such taxpayer services could include, but are not limited to, the following:

- the provision of readily accessible and easily understood local guidance on the domestic VAT rules that fall within the scope of the Guidelines;

- the creation of points of contact with taxing authorities where businesses and consumers can make inquiries regarding the domestic VAT rules within the scope of the Guidelines and receive timely responses to such inquiries;

- the creation of a point of contact with tax authorities where businesses can identify perceived disparities in the interpretation or implementation of the principles of the Guidelines. Such information can notably support the development of additional guidance on "best practices" or recommended approaches under the auspices of the CFA and its subsidiary bodies, as set out in paragraph 4.11 above.

4.19   Such initiatives are likely to reduce possible differences in the understanding of the Guidelines, enhance administrative consistency, and lower the probability of disputes. Jurisdictions are therefore encouraged to provide taxpayer services designed to facilitate a consistent interpretation of the Guidelines on neutrality and on place of taxation, when provision of such services is not inconsistent with national law or practice.

4.20   Jurisdictions have a variety of existing tax administration procedures for interpreting domestic law, including, in some jurisdictions, national advance ruling procedures. Jurisdictions are encouraged to take account of the Guidelines in interpreting domestic law through such existing procedures, including advance ruling procedures when they are available.

4.21   In connection with the development of taxpayer service initiatives directed at the Guidelines, tax authorities might look to the OECD's Forum on Tax Administration (FTA). Created by the CFA in 2002, the FTA is a forum for co-operation and the development of new ideas and approaches, including aspects of service delivery, to enhance tax administration throughout the world. The FTA's work program is supported by several subgroups and specialist networks, and it produces a variety of materials highlighting developments and trends in tax administration and providing practical guidance for tax authorities on important tax system management issues.

D. Application of the Guidelines in cases of evasion and avoidance

4.22   The Guidelines on neutrality and on place of taxation and the related commentaries apply when parties involved act in good faith and all transactions are legitimate and with economic substance.

4.23   In response to, or to prevent, evasion or avoidance, it is not inconsistent with the Guidelines for jurisdictions to take proportionate measures to protect against evasion and avoidance, revenue losses and distortion of competition.

4.24   This section is concerned with evasion and avoidance only in the context of these Guidelines. It is not intended to provide more general guidance on the concept of evasion or avoidance, or on jurisdictions' overall anti-evasion or anti-avoidance policies.

D.1. Meaning of evasion and avoidance

4.25   There are no common OECD definitions of the terms evasion and avoidance. However, these concepts are covered in the OECD's *Glossary of Tax Terms*,[54] as follows:

> **Evasion:** A term that is difficult to define but which is generally used to mean illegal arrangements where liability to tax is hidden or ignored, i.e. the taxpayer pays less tax than he is legally obligated to pay by hiding income or information from tax authorities.

> **Avoidance:** A term used to describe an arrangement of a taxpayer's affairs that is intended to reduce his liability and that although the arrangement could be strictly legal it is usually in contradiction with the intent of the law it purports to follow.

4.26   In the context of the Guidelines, the foregoing definitions are used for illustrative purposes only. They might not reflect the specific definitions that may exist in a national context or beyond the application of rules based on an interpretation of the Guidelines.

D.2. Illustration of the concepts of evasion and avoidance in a VAT context

4.27   Evasion could include the falsification or suppression of evidence or making false statements that result in VAT not being remitted to governments or that lead to inappropriate refunds being obtained from governments.

4.28   Avoidance could include situations resulting in a VAT advantage that is contrary to the intention of a law that is consistent with the Guidelines. Indications of VAT avoidance could include transactions that have been entered into solely or primarily to avoid VAT, or to gain a VAT advantage, and that are artificial, contrived, or lack economic substance. However, advantages provided for by law would not be deemed avoidance unless they are exploited to achieve an unintended result.

---

54. *www.oecd.org/ctp/glossaryoftaxterms.htm.*

APPENDIX

Recommendation of the Council on the application of value added tax/goods and services tax to the international trade in services and intangibles as approved on 27 September 2016 [C(2016)120]

THE COUNCIL,

HAVING REGARD to Article 5 b) of the Convention on the Organisation for Economic Co-operation and Development of 14 December 1960;

CONSIDERING that Value Added Tax (VAT)/Goods and Services Tax (GST) regimes have been implemented by countries around the world and that international trade in goods and services has likewise expanded rapidly in an increasingly globalised economy;

Considering that most world trade is subject to VAT/GST and that the interaction of VAT/GST regimes can have a major impact in either facilitating or distorting trade;

Considering that the absence of international VAT/GST coordination creates uncertainty and risks of double taxation and unintended non-taxation, hindering economic growth and business activity and distorting competition;

Considering that internationally agreed principles are needed on the application of VAT/GST to international trade to minimise the uncertainty and risks of double taxation and unintended non-taxation that result from inconsistencies in the application of VAT/GST in a cross-border context;

HAVING REGARD to the International VAT/GST Guidelines (hereinafter referred to as "the Guidelines") approved by the Committee on Fiscal Affairs on 7 July 2015 [CTPA/CFA(2015)57] and endorsed by the high level officials of 104 jurisdictions and international organisations at the third meeting of the OECD Global Forum on VAT on 5-6 November 2015, which set forth common principles for the consistent VAT/GST treatment of the most common types of international transactions, focusing on trade in services and intangibles;

NOTING that these Guidelines build on the generally accepted principles of VAT/GST neutrality and the destination principle for determining the place of taxation;

HAVING REGARD to the 2015 Final Report on Action 1 "Addressing the Tax Challenges of the Digital Economy" of the OECD/G20 Base Erosion and Profit Shifting (BEPS) Project, which was part of the BEPS package endorsed by the Council on 1 October 2015 [C(2015)125/ADD1] and by the G20 Leaders on 15-16 November 2015 and which includes the principles and collection mechanisms recommended by the Guidelines to address the BEPS risks and broader indirect tax challenges raised by the digital economy;

WELCOMING the inclusive and open consultative process for the development of the Guidelines with the participation of a broad range of stakeholders;

CONSIDERING that the Guidelines have gained worldwide recognition as an important reference point for designing and implementing VAT/GST legislation with a view to minimising the potential for double taxation and unintended non-taxation;

MINDFUL that the Guidelines do not aim at detailed prescriptions for national legislation but provide guidance to jurisdictions in developing legislation with a view to facilitating a coherent application of national VAT/GST systems to international trade, taking into account their specific economic, legal, institutional, cultural and social circumstances and practices;

On the proposal of the Committee on Fiscal Affairs:

I. Agrees that for the purpose of the present Recommendation the following definitions are used:

- **Value Added Tax (VAT)** refers to any national tax by whatever name or acronym it is known, such as Goods and Services Tax (GST), which embodies the basic features of a value added tax, i.e. a broad-based tax on final consumption collected from, but in principle not borne by, businesses through a staged collection process, whatever method is used for determining the tax liability (e.g. invoice-credit method or subtraction method);

- **Supplies of intangibles** refer to categories of supplies other than supplies of goods or services, such as supplies of intellectual property rights and other intangibles;

- **The principles of VAT neutrality** refer to the basic principles underpinning the neutrality of VAT for businesses, which is a necessary corollary of the basic definition of a VAT as a tax on final consumption that is collected from but in principle not borne by businesses. The concept of tax neutrality in VAT has a number of dimensions, including the absence of discrimination and the elimination of undue tax burdens and disproportionate or inappropriate compliance costs for businesses;

- **The destination principle** refers to the principle whereby, for consumption tax purposes, internationally traded services and intangibles should be taxed according to the rules of the jurisdiction of consumption.

II. Recommends that Members and non-Members adhering to this Recommendation (hereafter the "Adherents") take due account of the Guidelines, which are set out in the Appendix to this Recommendation and form an integral part thereof, when designing and implementing legislation with a view to minimising the potential for double taxation and unintended non-taxation in the application of VAT to the international trade in services and intangibles. To that effect, Adherents should in particular:

i) pursue efforts to implement the principles of VAT neutrality and the principles for determining the place of taxation of cross-border supplies in accordance with the destination principle set forth in the Guidelines when developing VAT legislation;

ii) use the Guidelines as a source of reference when applying the principles of VAT neutrality and the destination principle in practice, with a view to facilitating a coherent application of national VAT legislation to international trade;

III. INVITES Adherents and the Secretary-General to disseminate this Recommendation widely and utilise it as a tool for knowledge and experience sharing, regional co-operation programmes and dialogues and multilateral discussions on international VAT-related policies;

IV. INVITES non-Adherents to take due account of and to adhere to this Recommendation;

V. INVITES Adherents to support efforts for capacity building and assistance notably to developing countries so that they may be able to participate in and enjoy the benefits of these Guidelines;

VI. INSTRUCTS the Committee on Fiscal Affairs, through the Working Party No. 9 on Consumption Taxes, to:

i) monitor the implementation of the Recommendation and to report to Council no later than five years following its adoption and as appropriate thereafter;

ii) review and propose amendments of the Guidelines to Council, as appropriate, in the light of experience gained by Adherents and in consultation with relevant stakeholders;

iii) seek to improve clarity and certainty in the application of the Guidelines and consider work in related areas that have emerged in the course of the development of the Guidelines.

ORGANISATION FOR ECONOMIC CO-OPERATION AND DEVELOPMENT

The OECD is a unique forum where governments work together to address the economic, social and environmental challenges of globalisation. The OECD is also at the forefront of efforts to understand and to help governments respond to new developments and concerns, such as corporate governance, the information economy and the challenges of an ageing population. The Organisation provides a setting where governments can compare policy experiences, seek answers to common problems, identify good practice and work to co-ordinate domestic and international policies.

The OECD member countries are: Australia, Austria, Belgium, Canada, Chile, the Czech Republic, Denmark, Estonia, Finland, France, Germany, Greece, Hungary, Iceland, Ireland, Israel, Italy, Japan, Korea, Luxembourg, Mexico, the Netherlands, New Zealand, Norway, Poland, Portugal, the Slovak Republic, Slovenia, Spain, Sweden, Switzerland, Turkey, the United Kingdom and the United States. The European Union takes part in the work of the OECD.

OECD Publishing disseminates widely the results of the Organisation's statistics gathering and research on economic, social and environmental issues, as well as the conventions, guidelines and standards agreed by its members.

OECD PUBLISHING, 2, rue André-Pascal, 75775 PARIS CEDEX 16
(23 2017 03 1 P) ISBN 978-92-64-27204-0 – 2017

Printed in Great Britain
by Amazon